Joseph Gurney, Assizes, Lancashire Great Britain

The Whole Proceedings on the Trial of Indictment Against Thomas Walker of Manchester, Merchant

Samuel Jackson, James Cheetham, Oliver Pearsal, Benjamin Booth, and Joseph Collier, for a conspiracy to overthrow the constitution and government

Joseph Gurney, Assizes, Lancashire Great Britain

The Whole Proceedings on the Trial of Indictment Against Thomas Walker of Manchester, Merchant

Samuel Jackson, James Cheetham, Oliver Pearsal, Benjamin Booth, and Joseph Collier, for a conspiracy to overthrow the constitution and government

ISBN/EAN: 9783337734169

Printed in Europe, USA, Canada, Australia, Japan

Cover: Foto ©Suzi / pixelio.de

More available books at **www.hansebooks.com**

THE WHOLE PROCEEDINGS

ON THE

TRIAL OF INDICTMENT

AGAINST

THOMAS WALKER OF MANCHESTER,
MERCHANT,

SAMUEL JACKSON, JAMES CHEETHAM,
OLIVER PEARSAL, BENJAMIN BOOTH,

AND

JOSEPH COLLIER;

FOR

A CONSPIRACY TO OVERTHROW THE CONSTITUTION
AND GOVERNMENT.

AND

TO AID AND ASSIST THE FRENCH,

(being the King's Enemies)

IN CASE THEY SHOULD INVADE THIS KINGDOM.

TRIED

At the Assizes at Lancaster,

APRIL 2, 1794,

BEFORE THE HON. MR. JUSTICE HEATH,

ONE OF THE JUDGES

OF HIS MAJESTY'S COURT OF COMMON PLEAS.

———

TAKEN IN SHORT-HAND

BY JOSEPH GURNEY.

———

PHILADELPHIA:
PRINTED FOR SAMUEL HARRISON SMITH, BY W. WOODWARD.
1794.

CONTENTS.

THE indictment against Thomas Walker and others for a conspiracy - - - - - Page vii.
The indictment against Thomas Walker for seditious words - ix.
The indictment against James Cheetham for seditious words - xi.
List of the Grand Jury who found the bills of indictment - xii.
List of the Jury before whom the indictments were tried - xii.
———— Counsel - - - - - xii.
Mr. Law's Speech - - - - 13.
Evidence of Thomas Dunn - - - 19, 89.
———— Thomas Kinnaston - - - 33.
Mr. Erskine's Speech - - - - 36.
Evidence of Mr. George Wakefield - - - 52.
———— of George Clark - - - 57.
———— of James Lomax - - - 65.
———— of James Roberts - - - 69.
———— of Mary Denham - - - 71.
———— of Martha Wilkinson - - - 73.
———— of Francis Roberts - - - 76.
———— of Mr. Edward Green - - - 79.
———— of Mr. George Duckworth - - 83, 92.
———— of Mr. William Seddon - - 87, 91.
———— of John Spink - - - 93.
———— of John Twiss - - - 97.
———— of Mr. Thomas Jones - - - 100.
Lists of the Grand Jury who found the bill of indictment against Dunn for perjury - - - - 104.

APPENDIX.

Mr. Walker's first letter to Mr. Dundas - - i.
Mr. Walker's second letter to Mr. Dundas - - ii.
Mr. Walker's Letter to Mr. Wharton - - - iii.
Mr. Wharton's answer to Mr. Walker - - iii.
Mr. Walker's third letter to Mr. Dundas - iv.
The first subpœna with which Mr. Dundas was served - v.
The second subpœna with which Mr. Dundas was served - vi.
Mr. White's letter to Messrs. Ward, Dennetts, and Greaves - vii.
Particulars

CONTENTS.

Particulars of several applications made by Mr. Richard Walker to the Rev. John Griffith - - - viii.
Copy of a paper read by Mr. Richard Walker to the Rev. John Griffith, upon the 18th of July 1793 - - ix.
Copy of the paper signed A Reformer - - x.
Case of William Paul - - - xii.
The warrant by which Mr. Paul was apprehended - xii.
Mr. Paul's commitment to Lancaster - - xiii.
Case of Samuel Jackson - - - - xiii.
——— James Cheetham - - - xiv.
——— Oliver Pearsall - - - xiv.
——— Benjamin Booth - - - - xvi.
Copy of his pardon - - - - xvii.
Copy of a letter from Mr. Cartwright, a nonjuring bishop at Shrewsbury, to Benjamin Booth - - - xviii.

THE following pages contain the acount of a Trial, for a Conspiracy against the constitution and government of this kingdom in which I have been made the principal defendant. The reader, however, will observe, that some circumstances occurred in the course of these proceedings which give them the complexion of a conspiracy AGAINST the *Defendants;* myself in particular.

For the present at least, I shall only briefly state, that no falsehood or slander was too base or malignant, for my *persecutors* and their adherents, to invent and propagate, for the purpose of injuring my reputation, both as a merchant and as a man; nor was any attempt omitted that could irritate the public mind against myself and the other defendants; and consequently prejudge our cause.

When the rights of the public are attacked in the persons of individuals, the public are, (and ought to *feel*) deeply interested in the rise, the progress, and the event of the conflict. I am in possession of a series of facts, which for this reason I doubt not would be deemed important, not only to myself, but, at least, equally so to the public, and would illustrate, in some degree, the confession of Dunn (the evidence for the prosecution) that he was BRIBED to become my accuser.

Perhaps the secret movers of this iniquitous conspiracy may be traced, by tracing the conduct of their inferior agents: but the present publication would have been too long delayed, too much extended, and too miscellaneous, had the details been entered into, which

B were

were neceffary to apprife the public of the progrefs of the perfecution, with which the Defendants in this Trial have been haraffed.

But they fhall not be forgotten. I may at fome future time, if my health and my leifure will permit, give a fequel to this trial, which I have no doubt will throw fome light on the fecret machinations, and the open violence, alternately practifed againft the Friends of the People.

THOMAS WALKER.

MANCHESTER,
June 28, 1794.

Copy

Copy of the Indictment against Thomas Walker and others.

LANCASHIRE } THE Jurors for our Lord the King upon their
to wit   oath present that *Thomas Walker** late of *Manchester* in the county of *Lancaster* merchant; *George M'Cullum* late of the same place labourer, *John Smith* late of the same place labourer *William Paul* † late of the same place paper-stainer *Samuel Jackson* ‡ late of the same place chapman *James Cheetham* ‖ late of *Salford* in the said county labourer *Oliver Pearson* ** late of *Manchester* aforesaid labourer *Benjamin Booth* †† late of the same place labourer *Henry York* late of the same place gentleman and *Joseph Collier* late of the same place surgeon being wicked seditious and ill-disposed persons and disaffected to our Sovereign Lord the now king and the constitution and government of this kingdom as by law established and unlawfully contriving and intending as much as in them lay to break the peace and disturb the tranquillity of this kingdom did on the *first day of November* in the thirty-third year of the reign of our said present Sovereign Lord the now King *and on divers other days and times between that day and the twelfth day of June then next following* with force and arms at *Manchester* aforesaid in the county of *Lancaster* aforesaid

---

* There was a warrant on a charge of HIGH TREASON issued against, but not executed upon, this defendant: for the proceedings upon which, see the Appendix, No. I. to XI.

† There was a warrant of HIGH TREASON *executed* upon this defendant, for which, and for his treatment, see the Appendix No. XIII. XIV. and XV.

‡ There appears to have been a warrant for HIGH TREASON against this defendant issued and not executed, see Appendix No. XVI. This warrant, as well as those before-mentioned, was issued by the Rev. JOHN GRIFFITH, one of his Majesty's justices of the peace (at that time one of the chaplains to the collegiate church in Manchester, since elected a fellow thereof) upon the *sole* information of THOMAS DUNN, and for the *same accusations*, which are charged in this indictment as a conspiracy.

‖ For the treatment of this defendant, see Appendix No. XVII.

** This defendant's name is Oliver Pearsall, for the treatment he experienced, see the Appendix No. XVIII.

†† For this defendant's case, see the Appendix No. XIX.

Cheetham, Pearsal, and Booth, were all committed by the REVEREND JOHN GRIFFITH upon the *sole* information of THOMAS DUNN.

B 2

aforesaid unlawfully maliciously and seditiously, conspire combine and confederate with each other and also with divers disaffected and ill-disposed subjects of our said Lord the King whose names are to the Jurors at present unknown *to overthrow the constitution and government of this kingdom as by law established and to aid and assist the French then and there being enemies to and in open war with our said Lord the King against our said Lord the King in case such enemies should enter into and invade this kingdom in a warlike and hostile manner* and the said Thomas Walker George M'Cullum John Smith William Paul Samuel Jackson James Cheetham Oliver Pearson Benjamin Booth Henry York and Joseph Collier, in pursuance of the said conspiracy combination and agreement did on those several days and times at Manchester aforesaid in the county aforesaid *cause incite and encourage divers disaffected and ill-disposed subjects to the Jurors aforesaid unknown to learn and practice and to be instructed in the use of arms and military exercises for the purpose of assisting his said Majesty's said enemies against his said Majesty in case they should enter into and invade this kingdom* in contempt of our said Lord the King and his laws to the evil and pernicious example of all others in the like case offending and against the peace of our said Lord the King his crown and dignity And the Jurors aforesaid upon their oath aforesaid do further present that the said Thomas Walker George M' Cullum John Smith William Paul Samuel Jackson James Cheetham Oliver Pearson Benjamin Booth Henry York and Joseph Collier so being such persons as aforesaid and so contriving and intending as aforesaid did *on the said first day of November* in the thirty-third year aforesaid *and on divers other days and times between that day and the twelfth day of June* then next following with force and arms at Manchester aforesaid in the county aforesaid unlawfully maliciously and seditiously conspire combine and confederate with each other and also with divers disaffected and ill-disposed subjects of our said Lord the King whose names are to the said jurors at present unknown *to overthrow by force and arms the constitution and government of this kingdom as by law established.* And the said Thomas Walker George M'Cullum John Smith William Paul Samuel Jackson James Cheetham Oliver Pearson Benjamin Booth Henry York and Joseph Collier in pursuance of the said last-mentioned conspiracy combination and agreement did on those several days and times at Manchester aforesaid in the county aforesaid cause incite and encourage divers disaffected and ill-disposed subjects to the Jurors aforesaid unknown *to learn and practice and to be instructed in the use of arms and military exercises for the purpose of overthrowing by force and arms the constitution and government of this kingdom as by law established* in contempt of our said Lord the King and his laws to the evil and pernicious example of all others in the like case offending and against the peace of our said Lord the King his crown and dignity And the Jurors aforesaid upon their oath aforesaid do further present that the said Thomas Walker George M'Cullum John Smith William Paul Samuel Jackson James Cheetham Oliver Pearson Benjamin Booth Henry York and Joseph Collier so being such persons as aforesaid and so contriving and intending as aforesaid did *on the said first day of November* in the thirty-third year aforesaid *and on divers other days and times between that day and the twelfth day of June* then next following with force and arms at Manchester aforesaid in the county aforesaid unlawfully maliciously and seditiously conspire combine and confederate with each other and also with divers disaffected and ill-disposed subjects of our said Lord the King whose names are to the said Jurors at present unknown *to raise and stir up an insurrection and rebellion of his Majesty's subjects against his said Majesty and to aid and assist in such resurrection and rebellion for the purpose of overthrowing by force and arms the constitution and government of this kingdom as by law established* in contempt of our said Lord the King and his laws to the evil and pernicious example of all others in the like case offending and against the peace of our said Lord the King his crown and dignity And the Jurors aforesaid upon their oath aforesaid do further present that the said *Thomas Walker George M*^{c}*Cullum John Smith William Paul Samuel Jackson James Cheetham Oliver Pearson Benjamin Booth Henry York and Joseph Collier* so being such persons as aforesaid and so contriving and intending as aforesaid did *on the said first day of November* in the thirty-third year aforesaid *and on divers other days and times between that day and the twelfth day of June* then next following with force and arms at *Manchester* aforesaid in the county aforesaid unlawfully maliciously and seditiously conspire combine and confederate with each other and also with divers disaffected and ill-disposed subjects of our said Lord the King whose names are to the said Jurors at present unknown UNLAWFULLY TO OVERTHROW THE CONSTITUTION AND GOVERNMENT OF THIS KINGDOM AS BY LAW ESTABLISHED in contempt of our said Lord the King and his laws to the evil and pernicious example of all others in the like case offending and against the peace of our said Lord the King his crown and dignity.

BATT

Witnesses
    THOMAS DUNN
    THOMAS KINNASTON

Copy of the Indictment against Thomas Walker.

LANCASHIRE } THE Jurors for our Lord the King upon their
  to wit   oath present that *Thomas Walker* late of *Manchester* in the county of Lancaster *merchant* being a pernicious seditious and ill-disposed person and greatly disaffected to our said Lord the King and contriving and intending to move and incite the liege subjects of our said Lord the King to hatred and dislike of the person of our said Lord the King on the first day of June in the thirty-third year of the reign of our said Lord the King at *Manchester* aforesaid in the county aforesaid in the presence and hearing of divers liege subjects of our said Lord the King maliciously and seditiously did utter publish and declare the words following of and concerning our said Lord the King that is to say *What are Kings damn the King* (meaning our said Lord the now King) *what is he* (meaning our said Lord the now King) *to us if I* (meaning the said *Thomas Walker*) *had him* (meaning our said Lord the King) *in my power I* (meaning the said
Thomas

Thomas Walker) *would as soon take his* (meaning our said Lord the King's) *head off as I* (meaning the said *Thomas Walker*) *would tear this paper* he the said *Thomas Walker* then and there tearing in pieces a piece of paper which he then and there had and held in his hand to the great scandal of our said Lord the King in contempt of our said Lord the King and his laws to the evil and pernicious example of all others in the like case offending and against the peace of our said Lord the King his crown and dignity And the Jurors aforesaid upon their oath aforesaid do further present that the said *Thomas Walker* so being such person as aforesaid and so contriving and intending as aforesaid afterwards to wit on the same day and year aforesaid at Manchester aforesaid in the county aforesaid in the presence and hearing of divers other liege subjects of our said Lord the King maliciously and seditiously did utter publish and declare the words following of and concerning our said Lord the King that is to say *Damn the King* (meaning our said Lord the King) to the great scandal of our said Lord the King in contempt of our said Lord the King and his laws to the evil and pernicious example of all others in the like case offending and against the peace of our said Lord the King his crown and dignity And the Jurors aforesaid upon their oath aforesaid do further present that the said *Thomas Walker* so being such person as aforesaid and so contriving and intending as aforesaid afterwards to wit on the same day and year aforesaid at Manchester aforesaid in the county aforesaid in the presence and hearing of divers other liege subjects of our said Lord the King maliciously and seditiously did utter publish and declare the words following of and concerning our said Lord the King that is to say *If I* (meaning the said *Thomas Walker*) *had him* (meaning our said Lord the King) *in my power I* (meaning the said *Thomas Walker*) *would as soon take his* (meaning our said Lord the King's) *head off as I would tear this peace of paper* he the said *Thomas Walker* then and there tearing a piece of paper which he then and there had in his hand to the great scandal of our said Lord the King in contempt of our said Lord the King and his laws to the evil and pernicious example of all others in the like case offending and against the peace of our said Lord the King his crown and dignity And the Jurors aforesaid upon their oath aforesaid do further present that the said *Thomas Walker* so being such person as aforesaid and so contriving and intending as aforesaid afterwards to wit on the same day and year aforesaid at Manchester aforesaid in the county aforesaid in the presence and hearing of divers other liege subject of our said Lord the King maliciously and seditiously did utter publish and declare the following of and concerning our said Lord the King that is to say *There ought to be no King* (meaning that there ought to be no King of this realm) to the great scandal of our said Lord the King in contempt of our said Lord the King and his laws to the evil and pernicious example of all others in the like case offending and against the peace of our Lord the King his crown and dignity

BATT

Witness
  THOMAS DUNN

Copy

Copy of Indictment against James Cheetham.

LANCASHIRE *to wit.* | THE Jurors for our Lord the King upon their oath present That *James Cheetham* late of *Salford* in the county of *Lancaster* labourer being a pernicious seditious and ill-disposed person and greatly disaffected to our said Lord the now King and contriving and intending to move and incite the liege subjects of our said Lord the King to hatred and dislike of the person of our said Lord the king on the *tenth day* of June in the thirty-third year of the reign of our said Lord the King at Manchester in the county of Lancaster aforesaid in the presence and hearing of divers liege subjects of our said Lord the King did utter publish and declare the words following of and concerning our said Lord the King that is to say *Damn the King* (meaning our said Lord the King) *I* (meaning himself the said *James Cheetham*) *wish he* (meaning our said Lord the King) *was in the New Bailey Prison instead of Benjamin Booth* to the great scandal of our said Lord the King in contempt of our said Lord the King and his laws to the evil and pernicious example of all others in the like case offending and against the peace of our said Lord the King his crown and dignity And the jurors aforesaid upon their oath aforesaid do further present that the said *James Cheetham* so being such person as aforesaid and so contriving and intending as aforesaid afterwards (to wit) on the same day and year aforesaid at *Manchester* aforesaid in the county aforesaid in the presence and hearing of divers other liege subjects of our said Lord the King by whom the word guillotined hereafter mentioned was understood to mean put to death did utter publish and declare the words following of and concerning our said Lord the King (that is to say) *I* (meaning himself the said James Cheetham) *wish he* (meaning our said Lord the King) *was guillotined* (meaning put to death) to the great scandal of our said Lord the King in contempt of our said Lord the King and his laws to the evil and pernicious example of all others in the like case offending and against the peace of our said Lord the King his crown and dignity And the Jurors aforesaid upon their oath aforesaid do further present that the said *James Cheetham* so being such person as aforesaid and so contriving and intending as aforesaid afterwards (to wit) on the same day and year aforesaid at *Manchester* aforesaid in the county aforesaid in the presence and hearing of divers other liege subjects of our said Lord the King did utter publish and declare the words following of and concerning our said Lord the King that is to say " damn the King" (meaning our said Lord the King) to the great scandal of our said Lord the King to the evil and pernicious example of all others in the like case offending and against the peace of our said Lord the King his crown and dignity

BATT

Witness
 THOMAS DUNN

The three preceding Indictments were found by the Grand Jury of which the following is a List.

Sir Henry Hoghton, Baronet, of Hoghton, Foreman.
Thomas Butterworth Bayley, Esq. of Hope.
Henry Blundell, Esq. of Liverpool.
William Bankes, Esq. of Winstanley.
Samuel Bailey, Esq. of Lancaster.
Richard Crosse, Esq. of Adlington.
Robert Fletcher, Esq. of Preston.
Henry Philip Hoghton, Esq. of Hoghton.
Daniel Hoghton, Esq. of same.
Edward Gregg Hopwood, Esq. of Hopwood.
Geoffrey Hornby, Sen. Esq. of Preston.
William Hulton, Esq. of Hulton.
Bold Fleetwood Hesketh, Esq. of Rossal.
Abraham Rawlinson, Esq. of Ellel-hall.
William Rawlinson, Esq. of Ancoats.
Thomas Saul, Esq. of Lancaster.
Richard Shawe, Esq. of Preston.
Thomas Starkie, Esq. of Frenchwood.
Clayton Tarleton, Esq. of Liverpool.
Daniel Wilson, Esq. of Dalham Tower.

ASSIZES AT LANCASTER,
April 2d, 1794,
Before the Hon. Mr. Justice Heath.

JURY.

William Harper, of Everton.
Edward Entwisle, of Damend, in Ribchester.
John Jolly, of Mythop.
Richard Dixon, of Poulton.
John Ellison, of Liverpool.
James Parke, of Presall.
Alexander Tomlinson, of Oswaldtwistle.
John Williamson, of Scotforth.
John Carter, of Hambleton.
William Culshaw, of North Meols.
Nicholas Heys, of Upholland.
Joseph Brown, of Poulton.

Counsel for the Crown.
Mr Law, Attorney-General for the County Palatine of Lancaster.
Mr. Wood.
Mr. Topping.
Mr. Johnson.
Mr. James.

Counsel for the Defendants.
The Hon. Thomas Erskine.
Mr. Serjeant Cockell.
Mr. Chambre.
Mr. Lloyd.
Mr. Felix Vaughan.

Solicitor.
Mr. White, Solicitor to the Treasury.

Solicitors.
Messrs Duckworth and Dennett.
Mr. William Seddon.

[*The Indictment was opened by Mr.* JAMES.]

Mr. LAW.

May it please your Lordship—Gentlemen of the Jury:

The indictment which has been read to you, imputes to the defendants a species of treasonable misdemeanor, second only in degree, and inferior only in malignity to the crime of high treason itself. It imputes to them a conspiracy for the purpose of adhering with effect to the King's enemies, in case the calamity of foreign invasion or of internal and domestic tumult should afford them the desired opportunity of so doing. A conspiracy for the purpose of employing against our country those arms which should be devoted to its defence; and of overthrowing a constitution, the work of long continued wisdom and virtue in the ages that have gone before us, and which, I trust, the sober minded virtue and wisdom of the present age will transmit unimpaired to ages that are yet to succeed us. It imputes to them a conspiracy, not indeed levelled at the person and life of our sovereign, but at that constitution at the head of which he is placed, and at that system of beneficial laws which it is his pride and his duty to administer; at that constitution which makes us what we are, a great, free, and I trust, with a few exceptions only, an happy and united people. Gentlemen, a conspiracy formed for these purposes, and to be effected eventually by means of arms; a conspiracy which had either for its immediate aim or probable consequence, the introduction into this country, upon the model of France, of all the miseries that disgrace and desolate that unhappy land, is the crime for which the defendants stand arraigned before you this day; and it is for you to say, in the first instance, and for my Lord hereafter, what shall be the result and effect in respect to persons against whom a conspiracy of such enormous magnitude and mischief shall be substantiated in evidence.

Gentlemen, whatever subjects of political difference may subsist amongst us, I trust we are in general agreed in venerating the great principles of our constitution, and in wishing to sustain and render them permanent. Whatever toleration and indulgence we may be willing to allow to differences in matters of less importance, upon some subjects we can allow none; for the friends of France, leagued in unity of council, inclination, and interest with France, against the arms and interests of this country, however tolerant in other respects, we can afford no grains of allowance, no sentiments of indulgence, or toleration whatsoever; to do so, particularly at a time when those arms and councils are directed against our political and civil, against not our national only, but our natural existence (and at such a period you will find that the very conspiracy now under consideration was formed), would be equally inconsistent with every rule of law and every principle of self-preservation: it would be at once to authorise every description of mischievous persons to carry their destructive principles into immediate and fatal effect; in other words, it would be to sign the doom and downfall of that constitution which protects us all.

I am sure, therefore, for the crime, such as I have represented it to be, my learned friend will not, in the exercise of his own good sense, choose to offer any defence or apology; but he will endeavour to make the evidence I shall lay before you appear in another point of view: he will endeavour to conceal and soften much of that malignity which I impute, and I think justly, to the intentions and actings of these defendants.

It was about the close of the year 1792, that the French nation thought fit to hold out to all the nations on the globe, or rather, I should say, to the discontented subjects of all those nations, an encouragement to confederate and combine together, for the purpose of subverting all regular established authority amongst them, by a decree of that nation of the 19th of November 1792, which I consider as the immediate source and origin of this and other mischievous societies. That nation, in convention, pledged to the discontented inhabitants of other countries, its protection and assistance, in case they should be disposed to innovate and change the form of government under which they had heretofore lived. Under the influence of this fostering encouragement, and meaning, I must suppose, to avail themselves of the protection and assistance thus held out to them, this and other dangerous societies sprung up, and spread themselves within the bosom of this realm.

Gentlemen, it was about the period I mentioned, or shortly after, I mean in the month of December, which followed close upon the promulgation of this detestable decree, that the society on which I am about to comment, and ten members of which are now presented in trial before you, was formed*. The vigilance of those to whom the administration of justice and the immediate care of the police of the country is primarily entrusted, had already prevented or dispersed every numerous assembly of persons which resorted to public-houses for such purposes; it therefore became necessary for persons thus disposed, to assemble themselves to do so, if at all, within the walls of some private mansion. The president and head of this society, Mr. Thomas Walker, raised to that bad eminence by a species of merit which will not meet with much favour or encouragement here, opened his doors to receive a society of this sort at Manchester, miscalled the Reformation Society: the name may, in some senses, indeed, import and be understood to mean a society formed for the purpose of beneficial reform; but what the real purposes of this society were, you will presently learn, from their declared sentiments and criminal actings. He opened his doors, then, to receive this society; they assembled, night after night, in numbers, to an amount which you will hear from the witnesses. Sometimes, I believe, the extended number of such assemblies amounting to more than a hundred persons. There were three considerable rooms allotted for their reception. In the lower part of the house, where they were first admitted, they

---

* The Manchester Constitutional Society was instituted in October 1790. The Reformation Society in March 1792. The Patriotic Society in April 1792.

fat upon bufinefs of lefs moment, and requiring the prefence of fmaller numbers; in the upper part, they affembled in greater multitudes, and read, as in a fchool, and as it were to fafhion and perfect themfelves in every thing that is feditious and mifchievous, thofe writings which have been already reprobated by other juries fitting in this and other places, by the courts of law, and in effect, by the united voice of both houfes of parliament. They read, amongft other works, particularly, the works of an author, whofe name is in the mouth of every body in this country; I mean the works of Thomas Paine; an author, who, in the gloom of a French prifon, is now contemplating the full effects and experiencing all the miferies of that diforganizing fyftem of which he is, in fome refpect, the parent—certainly the great advocate and promoter.

The works of this author, and many other works of a fimilar tendency, were read aloud by a perfon of the name of Jackfon, who exercifed upon thofe occafions the mifchievous function of reader to this fociety. Others of the defendants had different functions affigned them; fome were bufied in training them to the ufe of arms, for the purpofe, avowedly, in cafe there fhould be either a landing of the French, with whom we were then, I think, actually at war, or about to be immediately at war; or in cafe there fhould take place a revolt in the kingdoms of Ireland or Scotland, to minifter to their affiftance, either to fuch invafion or to fuch revolt. That they met for fuch purpofes is not only clear from the writings that were read aloud to them, and the converfations that were held, but by the purpofes which were exprefsly declared and avowed by thofe who may be confidered as the mouthpieces and organs of the fociety upon thefe occafions.

The firft time, I think, that the witnefs Dunn, whom I fhall prefently produce to you, faw the defendant Mr. Walker, Mr. Walker declared to him, *" that he hoped they fhould foon overthrow the conflitution."* The witnefs I have alluded to, was introduced to the fociety by two perfons, I think of the names of M'Callum and Smith, and who, if I am not mifinformed, have fince taken their flight from this country to America. The firft night he was there, he did not fee their prefident, Mr. Walker, but on the fecond night that he went there, Mr. Walker met him as he entered the door, and obferving, from his dialect, that he was a native of Ireland, Mr. Walker enquired of him how the volunteers went on, and faid, with a fmile, as he paffed him in his way up ftairs to the reft of the affociated members, *" we fhall overthrow the conflitution by " and by."* The witnefs was then ufhered into this room, where he faw affembled nearly to the number of an hundred or an hundred and fifty perfons. The room was, I underftand, a large warehoufe at the top of the houfe; there were about fourteen or fifteen perfons then actually under arms, and fome of thofe whofe names are to be found in this record, were employed in teaching others the military exercife. It would be endlefs, as well as ufelefs, to relate to you the whole of what paffed at thefe feveral meetings.

Upon fome occafions, Mr. Walker would talk in the moft contumelious and abominable language of the facred perfon of our fovereign. In one inftance, when talking of monarchy, he faid,

"damn kings! what have we to do with them, what are they to
"us?" and, to shew the contempt in which he held the lives of
all kings, and particularly that of our own sovereign, taking a
piece of paper in his hand and tearing it, he said, "if I had the
"king here, I would cut off his head, as readily as I tear this
"paper."

Upon other occasions, others of the members, and particularly
a person of the name of Paul, who I believe is now in court, held
similar language: damning the king; reviling and defaming him
in the execution of his high office; representing the whole system of
our government as a system of plunder and rapacity; representing,
particularly, the administration of a neighbouring kingdom by a
lord lieutenant, as a scheme and device merely invented to corrupt
the people, and to enrich and aggrandize the individual to whose
care the government of that kingdom is more immediately delegated; in short, arraigning every part of our public œconomy as directly productive of misgovernment and oppression. The King
himself was sometimes more particularly pointed at by Mr. Walker. He related of him a strange, incredible, and foolish fable,
which I never heard suggested from any other quarter;—"That
"his Majesty was possessed of seventeen millions of money in some
"bank or other at Vienna, which he kept locked up there, and
"would not bestow a single penny of it to relieve the distresses and
"indigence of any part of his own subjects." Many other assertions of this sort were made, and conversations of a similar
import held, between Mr. Walker and the persons thus assembled.

About three months after the formation, as far as I can collect
it, of this society, that is, about the month of March 1793, a person of the name of Yorke; Yorke of Derby, I think he is called,
arrived at Manchester, with all the apparatus of a kind of apostolic mission, addressed to the various assemblies of seditious persons
in that quarter of the kingdom. He harangued them upon such topics as were most likely to interest and inflame them; he explained
to them the object of the journey he was then making through the
country; he said, he was come to visit all the combined societies,
in order to learn the numbers they could respectively muster, in
case there should be an invasion by the French, which was then
talked of, and is yet, I am afraid, talked of, but upon too much
foundation; to know, in short, what number they could add to the
arms of France, in case these arms should be hostilely directed
against Great Britian itself; he stated that the French were about
to land in this country to the number of forty or fifty thousand men,
and that he was collecting, in the different societies, the names of
such persons as could be best depended upon, in order to ascertain
what number in the whole could actually be brought into the field
upon such an emergency.

When this person was present, there seems to have been a sort of
holiday and festival of sedition: each member strove with his fellow
which should express sentiments the most injurious and hostile to the
peace and happiness of their country. Dunn, the witness I have already alluded to, will speak to the actual communication of all the several
persons who are defendants upon this record in most of the mis-

chievous councils which were then held, and which are the subject of this prosecution. They met during a considerable length of time he attended (and here you will not be called upon to give credit to a loose and casual recollection of a few random expressions, uttered upon one or two accidental occasions, capable of an innocent or doubtful construction), but he attended, I believe, at nearly forty of these meetings; he attended them from about the month of December or January, down to the month of June, when, either through compunction for the share he had himself borne in those mischievous proceedings, or whatever else might be his motive (I trust it was an honourable one, and that it will in its effects prove beneficial to his country), he came forward and detailed this business to the magistrates of this county. It became them, having such circumstances related to them, and having it also confirmed by other evidence, that there were numerous nightly meetings of this sort held at stated intervals at the house of Mr. Walker, upon having the objects of these meetings detailed and verified to them, it became them, I say, to use means for suppressing a mischief of such extent and magnitude. It was accordingly thought proper to institute this prosecution for the purpose of bringing these enormous proceedings into public discussion and enquiry, before a jury of the country, and for the purpose of eventually bringing to condign punishment the persons immediately concerned in them.

Gentlemen, the evidence of this person, the witness I have mentioned, will unquestionably be assailed and attacked by a great deal of attempted contradiction; his character will, I have no doubt, be arraigned and drawn in question from the earliest period to which the defendants can have any opportunities of access, for materials respecting it. Upon nothing but upon the effectual impeachment of the character of this witness, can they bottom any probable expectations of acquittal; to that point, therefore, their efforts will be mainly directed. I wish their efforts had been hitherto directed innocently towards the attainment of this object, and that no opportunities had been recently taken in occasional meetings and conversations to attempt to tamper with the testimony of this witness. There are other practices, which next to an actual tampering with the testimony of a witness, are extremely mischievous to the regular course and administration of justice. I mean attempts to lure a witness into conversations respecting the subject of his testimony; of this we have seen many very blameable instances in the course of the present circuit, where conversations have been set on foot for the purpose of catching at some particular expressions, inadvertently dropt by a witness, and of afterwards bringing them forward, separately and detached from the rest of the conversation, in order to give a different colour and complexion to the substance of his evidence, and to weaken the effect and credit of the whole.

Gentlemen, these attempts are too commonly made; happily, however, for public justice, they are commonly unsuccessful; because they do and must, with every honourable mind, recoil upon the party making them. Private applications to a person not only known to be an adverse witness, but to be the very witness upon whose credit the prosecution most materially depends; private conversations with such a witness, for the purpose of getting from him declarations which may be afterwards opposed in seeming contradiction to his solemn testimony upon oath, are of themselves so dishonourable that with every well-disposed and well-judging mind, they will naturally produce an effect directly contrary to the expectations of the persons who make them.

I know, Gentlemen, what I have most to fear upon this occasion; I know the vigour and energy of the mind of my learned friend. I have long felt and admired the powerful effect of his various talents. I know the ingenious sophistry by which he can mislead, and the fascination of that eloquence by which he can subdue the minds of those to whom he addresses himself. I know what he can do to-day, by seeing what he has done upon many other occasions before. But, at the same time, Gentlemen, knowing what he is, I am somewhat consoled in knowing you. I have practised for several years in this place; I know the sound discretion and judgment by which your verdicts are generally governed, and upon the credit of that experience, I trust that it will not be in the power of my friend, by any arts he is able to employ, to seduce you a single step from the sober paths of truth and justice. You will hear the evidence with the attention which becomes men who are deciding on the fate of others. If these defendants be innocent, and my learned friend is able to substantiate their innocence, to your satisfaction, for God's sake let them be acquitted; but if that innocence cannot be clearly and satisfactorily established, I stand here interested as I am in common with him in the acquittal of innocence, at the same time however demanding the rights of public justice against the guilty. It imports the safety of yourselves, it imports the safety of our country, it imports the existence and security of every thing that is dear to us; if these men be not innocent, that no considerations of tenderness and humanity, no considerations of any sort short of what the actual abstract justice of the case may require, should prevent the hand of punishment from falling heavy on them.

Having, therefore, Gentlemen, given you this short detail and explanation of the principal facts which are about to be laid before you in evidence, I will now close the trouble I mean to give you, in the first instance. I shall by and by, when my learned friend has adduced that evidence by which he will attempt to assail the character and credit of the principal witness for the prosecution, have an opportunity of addressing you again; and, I trust, in the mean time, that whatever attention you may be disposed to pay to the exertions of those who will labour to establish the innocence of the persons now arraigned before you, that you will, at the same time, steadily bear in mind the duties which you owe to yourselves and to your country; recollecting, as I am sure you will, that we all look up to your firmness and integrity at this moment, for the protection of that constitution from which we derive every blessing we individually or collectively enjoy.

EVIDENCE FOR THE CROWN.

Thomas Dunn, (sworn.)

Examined by Mr. *Wood*.

Q. I believe you are a weaver, and live at Manchester?
A. Yes.
Q. Were you at any time introduced to any society at Mr. Walker's house there?
A. Yes, I was.
Q. Do you recollect when it was?
A. I believe in the latter end of September, in the year 1792.
Q. Who was you introduced by?
A. M'Callum and Smith.
Q. What was this society called?
A. The Reformation Society.
Q. What is become of M'Callum and Smith?
A. I cannot tell; the last time I saw them they told me they were going to America.
Q. What number of people might there be when you was first introduced?
A. Sometimes there were more, sometimes less; I cannot tell to the exact number.
Q. How many do you think there were the first time when you were introduced by M'Callum and Smith?
A. Perhaps fifty or sixty.
Q. Were you all in the same room, or in different rooms?
A. In different rooms.
Q. How many different rooms might you be in?
A. In two, as far as I can recollect, that night.
Q. What was going forward in these different rooms?
A. As far as I could see there were politics spoken of, and other men were learning discipline.
Q. What had they to learn their discipline with?
A. Firelocks.
Q. How many might there be learning their discipline?
A. About six or seven.
Q. Was that in the room in which they were talking politics?
A. No, in a different room.
Q. Do you recollect what sort of politics were talked?
A. They were reading a paper; I cannot exactly tell the words; the whole of the meeting was entirely with respect to a reformation in parliament; the motive was entirely that, as far as I could understand.
Q. Did you say the motive was entirely that?
A. Yes, as far as I could understand it that night.
Q. How long might you be there that night?
A. I cannot recollect the time; I never stopped above an hour or two there, my employ called me that I could not come there before

eight o'clock; I commonly went back again to get home about ten.

Q. When was the next time you was there?
A. I went there the Monday following.
Q. Was Monday the day of meeting?
A. Yes, the particular day.
Q. Did you see Mr. Walker at that time?
A. Not the firſt day, I did not; I ſaw him the ſecond time.
Q. Where did you ſee him?
A. I knocked at his door, and I met him at the door within the houſe.
Q. What did Mr. Walker ſay to you?
A. He wanted to know my buſineſs. I told him I wiſhed to go to the ſociety; he ſaid he perceived I was an Iriſhman: I ſaid, yes, I was; he ſaid, had I any account from Ireland lately, and how the Volunteers were going on? I told him I thought they were going on very proſperous; upon that he juſt waved his hand, and ſaid, *we would overthrow the conſtitution by and by;* upon that I went up to the ſociety room; there was a candle and candleſtick in every paſſage up the ſtairs.
Q. Did you ſee any body there?
A. Yes, a great many people.
Q. How many do you ſuppoſe there were at that time?
A. I think there might be above a hundred and fifty there that night.
Q. What were they doing?
A. Some one thing, ſome another; there were about fifteen or ſixteen under arms.
Q. What were they doing under arms?
A. Going through the manual exerciſe.
Q. Was there any body there to inſtruct them in it?
A. O yes, one Oliver Pearſall.
Q. Did Mr. Walker come among you?
A. Yes.
Q. Do you remember one Samuel Jackſon?
A. Yes.
Q. Was he there at this time?
A. I dont know but he might come there.
Q. Do you know whether he was there or not?
A. I actually cannot tell whether I ſaw him there at that time or not?
Q. Was there any thing done at that meeting except learning the exerciſe?
A. No.
Q. How long might you ſtay that night?
A. Not very long, I never ſtopped very long.
Q. Did you go again after that?
A. Yes, very often.
Q. Did you ſee Mr. Walker there?
A. Yes, every night; I never miſſed Mr. Walker but one night.
Q. Did you ever hear Mr. Walker ſay any thing relative to what was going forward there about theſe people learning the uſe of arms?
A. I do not know what you mean.

Q. You have said, there were people there learning their exercise.
A. Yes.
Q. Have you heard Mr. Walker say for what purpose it was?
A. Yes, I have.
Q. What did he say?
A. I have heard him say so far as this, that it was his intention and the design was to forward and to aid the French, if they would land here.
Q. Do you know Cheetham?
A. Yes, very well?
Q. And Booth?
A. Yes.
Q. Did you see them there?
A. Yes.
Q. And Paul?
A. Yes, I saw him there.
Q. Did you see them there frequently, or only once, or twice?
A. Frequently.
Q. Did you see Collier there?
A. I did.
Q. Have you ever seen Jackson at any of those meetings?
A. O yes, he was a very great reader in politics.
Q. Did he read to the people that were there?
A. Yes.
Q. What sort of books might he read?
A. Paine's Works, and a man, I forget him now, and Cooper's Reply to Mr. Burke's Invective, and other matters; he always had something new.
Q. Was it declared what was the intent of this society?
A. I absolutely just will inform you, candidly, in my opinion, as far as I can learn, when I came to understand myself properly, that it was to overthrow the whole constitution?
Q. Did you understand it so?
A. I understand it so now, but not at that time.
Q. What did you understand then was the object and design of this meeting?
A. I understood at that time that it was to serve poor people.
Q. How were the poor people to be served?
A. By association together, I thought, and to have so far as this to be neighbourly, and no further; I thought so.
Q. Did you ever hear any thing said about the Irish or the Scotch?
A. At what time?
Q. At any of those meetings?
A. Yes, I did.
Q. What was said about them?
A. I recollect to hear a letter read, an address from the United Irishmen to Scotland.
Q. Who read that?
A. Mr. Paul, I think, to the best of my recollection; it was either he, or Jeakson; but however, Mr. Paul came out with these expressions, which I will relate to the whole court; the matter stood thus, when the letter was read I cannot say, whether he or

Paul might read it himſelf I cannot pretend to ſay, but Mr. Paul ſaid, that if ever we ſhould have a revolt, it would be, from the Iriſh; he ſays, I have property in Ireland myſelf, and he wondered the Iriſhmen there mentioned did not exert themſelves more than they did do: I happened to be the very next man to him, I ſaid, I am an Iriſhman myſelf; he ſaid, I know you are, he ſaid, if ever we ſhould have a revolt, it ſhould be through the Iriſh; they have ſent a deputy to Ireland as a King; damn him, ſaid he, and all Kings.

Q. Do you remember Mr. Yorke—Henry Yorke?
A. Yes, I do; I will not pretend to ſay that I ſhould know the man; I never ſaw him but one night for about an hour.
Q. Who was he introduced by?
A. By Mr. Thomas Walker.
Q. What was he introduced for?
A. It was that very night that he happened to come, it happened to be very thin of people; but howſoever he was introduced, and took by his arm into our place; he was introduced as a Gentleman of the ſame principles; and all hands were put up that he ſhould be the chairman.
Q. And did he take the chair?
A. He did.
Q. What did he ſay to you?
A. He mentioned he was glad to ſee ſo many loyaliſts; he was glad to ſee ſo many friends; he had juſt come from Sheffield; he ſaid he was only a ſhort time from France; that he lay a fortnight in Paine's houſe in Paris. At this time there were different opinions, with reſpect to whether they ſhould draw up a petition to recommend for a reform; he ſaid, there was that height of petitions *(deſcribing it)* from Scotland and other parts.
Q. Had he thoſe petitions with him?
A. No, he told us it was ſo in Sheffield, different copies; he ſaid nothing will do but a reform—a reformation then was clapped—he ſaid, that he was going through the three kingdoms, to ſee what aid they could have to aſſiſt the French, if they ſhould land here.

Mr. *Erſkine*. Repeat that over again.
A. To aid and aſſiſt, to know the aid that might be for the French.

Mr. *Wood*. Did he ſay any thing about the number of French that might be expected?
A. Fifty thouſand.
Q. Were there a great many members preſent that night?
A. Not a great many, I cannot ſay the exact number; there might be about fifty, it was a very wet night, I recollect that.
Q. Was there any exerciſes learned that night?
A. Yes, there was.
Q. How many different meetings might you attend in all, think you?
A. I dare ſay forty or fifty, I can be ſafe upon that.
Q. Do you remember Benjamin Booth's being taken into cuſtody?
A. I do.

Q. Did you apply to the society upon that occasion?
A. I did.
Q. What was your application for him?
A. To get him some money.
Q. Did you get any money for him?
A. There was some money got for him that night.
Q. Do you remember being there at any other time, when there was any conversation about the King?
A. Many times; I do not suppose there was any night but there was something of that kind.
Q. Recollect something that was said about the King.
A. Upon what night?
Q. When any thing was said about the King?
A. I remember being there one night in particular, when Mr. Thomas Walker was speaking with respect to war; he disapproved of the war entirely, and he thought the ministry was highly to blame, and the whole to involve us in a war. That he had seventeen millions of money in the bank of Vienna?
Q. Who had seventeen millions of money?
A. The King, in the bank of Vienna, and he would not give one penny to serve the poor; damn him, and all kings. He had a bit of paper in his hand; he said, he would as soon take his head off as he would that, and he tore the paper.
Q. Do you recollect how many people were present then?
A. I cannot pretend to say how many there were.
Q. Did you hear any thing said that night about Ireland?
A. I do not recollect I did.
Q. Did you hear him at any other time say any thing about Ireland? did you hear William Paul say any thing?
A. I mentioned that; I will say it over again, if you please.
Q. Do so.
A. There was an address of the United Irishmen to Scotland.
Q. You said that before; do you remember being at a meeting after the death of the late French King?
A. Yes.
Q. Who was there then?
A. A good many.
Q. Was Collier there?
A. Yes, he came in, we were discoursing the matter, and all rejoicing upon it; he came into the place; he thought he was the first, in one sense, to announce to the company that it was so; he passed round, he damned him, and wished all kings were served so.
Q. Do you remember whether Jackson recommended any thing to the meeting?
A. He recommended every thing to be very candid, and keep every thing very secret, that we should be unanimous one to another.
Q. Did you go openly and publicly to Mr. Walker's house?
A. No, latterly we went there as private as possible since.
Q. Which door did you go in at?
A. At the back door.
Q. Since what time was it that you went privately?

A. Since it was known so publicly, that we were called Painters, when we were turned out of the public-houses, that we could not meet there.

Q. Then you went to Mr. Walker's?
A. Yes, he opened that house for us.

Q. What door did you go in at?
A. The back door in general; I never went in at the front door in my life, but at the second time.

Q. Did others go in at the back door or not?
A. Some went in at the front, some at the back door.

Q. What were you afraid of?
A. I was afraid, as much as any thing, of the constables.

Q. Do you know whether they were watching you or not?
A. I knew they were.

Q. What constables were watching you?
A. The different constables of the town; I think the deputy of Salford was watching us as much as any body. Mr. Walker sent out different men to watch them; there are men in the bar, that if they would speak the truth, know they went out to watch them.

Thomas Dunn.

Cross-examined by Mr. Erskine.

Q. What is your Christian name?
A. Thomas Dunn.

Q. Why do you call it your Christian name?
A. I was brought up by that.

Q. Was you ever christened?
A. I hope so.

Q. Then you forgot that circumstance *formerly*—do you hear me?
A. Yes.

Q. You forgot that circumstance once of your having been christened.
A. Have I? how long since?

Q. Do you remember ever having been asked the question?
A. I remember you asked me what my name was, and I answered you that my name was Thomas Dunn.

Q. Was you never asked at any other time, and by any body else?
A. Very well, and suppose I choose to tell this or that.

Q. But you happened to be upon your oath at the time I am speaking of.
A. I am speaking now, that my name is Thomas Dunn, and upon my oath I am speaking, I know what you are upon Mr. Erskine; I tell you in this place, that I defy you, though the learned Mr. Erskine is come down here to insult me.

Mr. Justice *Heath.* You must behave properly.
A. I have served his majesty for years, and would serve him to day; is Mr. Erskine to disprove my name?

Mr. Justice *Heath.* You must not put yourself in a passion, but behave decently.

Mr. *Erskine.* I wish this worthy gentleman may be left to himself subject only to your Lordship's interposition when he misbehaves. You will find I am not so easily put out, as you fancy; therefore I will resume my question again: Was you never asked, when you was sworn to speak the truth, whether you had been christened or not, and what answer did you give?

A. No, never in my life.

Q. Do you mean to swear, that such a question was never put to you in a court of justice, when you came forward to convict one of these innocent men that you are now a witness against?

A. Innocent!

Q. That his Lordship and the Jury are to try. Was that question ever put to you, and did you give it any, and what answer? I am in no hurry; his Lordship will have the goodness to wait for you.

A. If you will speak the words over again.

Q. Was you never asked, when sworn upon the Gospels to speak the truth, whether you were christened or no, and what answer did yuo give?

A. I tell you I never was in my life.

Q. Never was what?

A. I never was asked whether I was christened or not*.

Q. You can read, I take it for granted?

A. No, I can neither read nor write.

Q. There is something wrote up there, *(opposite the witness box,)* which otherwise I would have recommended to your perusal? †

A. I am quite an illiterate man.

Q. Who was it that told you I was come down here for the purpose of insulting you?

A. What, Mr. Erskine.

Q. You seem perfectly familiar with my name.

A. Yes, and I know your person too.

Q. Who told you that?

A. No gentleman here told me.

Q. How came you to know?

A. I was acquainted the night before last where you lodged at Preston.

Q. Who told you so?

A. The landlord, that you and Mr. Walker were there together.

Q. You never knew any thing of me before that?

A. O yes, I saw you before; I know more of you than you fancy.

Q. Did you ever see me before or not?

---

* When Benjamin Booth was convicted at the Manchester Sessions, *upon Dunn's sole evidence,* Dunn was asked if he had ever been baptized; to which he replied in the negative.

† " Thou shalt not bear false witness against thy neighbour.',

A. I saw your picture.
Q. That is all?
A. Yes.
Q. Was that all you meant when you said you knew more of me than I fancied?
A. No, I could tell you more. *(Here Mr. Justice Heath interrupted Mr. Erskine by saying we have nothing to do with this.)*
Q. It was in the month of September you first went to this meeting?
A. I do not know but it might.
Q. Do you mean to swear that it was?
A. No, I do not mean to swear about it.
Q. Do you know what month it was in?
A. No.
Q. Do you know what year it was in?
A. In 1792.
Q. Do you remember the riot at Manchester?
A. Yes.
Q. When Mr. Walker's house was surrounded and attacked?
A. I remember to have heard of it.
Q. Was it before or after that?
A. After.
Q. You are certain of that?
A. Very certain.
Q. The first time you was at this society was after the riot?
A. Yes.
Q. How long do you think it might be after the riot, some weeks, was it not?
A. I think it was a few days.
Q. Are you quite sure it was after the riot?
A. Yes.
Q. And you think about a few days?
A. Yes.
Q. Which society did you belong to?
A. The Reformation Society.
Q. Was you elected into it, or did you go upon the invitation of any body?
A. I went upon the invitation of one Smith and M'Callum.
Q. Nobody else knew you there, of course, that constituted this society?
A. I knew two or three of them when I went in.
Q. The rest were strangers to you?
A. Yes.
Q. So much so, that you did not even know their names, nor they you?
A. I knew them by sight; their names I did not know.
Q. At the next meeting you saw Mr. Walker?
A. Yes.
Q. At the door of his house, I think you tell us, you met him. Was he acquainted with you, or you with him?
A. I never saw the man in my life before, not to know him.
Q. He found out that you were an Irishman by your tongue, of course?

A. Yes.
Q. And asked your business?
A. Yes.
Q. You told him you were going to the society?
A. Yes.
Q. Were Smith or M'Callum with you at that time?
A. No person but myself.
Q. Then Mr. Walker knew nothing of you but what you told him?
A. Just so.
Q. He asked you whether you had heard from Ireland lately about the Volunteers?
A. Yes.
Q. And immediately upon that he rapped out what you told us a little while ago about the constitution?
A. Yes.
Q. And then you went to the society, and Mr. Yorke took the chair?
A. It was not that night that Mr. Yorke took the chair.
Q. How long after was it that Mr. Yorke took the chair?
A. A very little time after.
Q. What passed the night of the day you saw Mr. Walker?
A. Nothing transpired more than was customary in the place.
Q. You said it appeared to you the object of the meeting was a reform of parliament for the benefit of the poor?
A. I thought so at the first go off, or I should never have joined it.
Q. You was not a man of those bad principles, was you?
A. I do not know what you may call bad principles.
Q. You was not a man that would wish to overthrow the constitution, was you?
A. No, I absolutely was not never to overturn it; I think we never could have a better.
Q. So I think too. Then you always was of that mind?
A. Yes, I was always of that principle.
Q. That it would be better to reform our constitution by petitions to parliament to reform it, than to overthrow it?
A. Yes, but I never saw a design of that in our society.
Q. You never saw a design to overturn the constitution?
A. No, I never saw any design, or the least motion moved to petition parliament for a reform.
Q. How many times did you attend?
A. I cannot tell the number; but I dare say forty or fifty.
Q. During all the time you met, what do you believe was the intention of these people?
A. I believed at the first go off, that it was for a reform; that a petition might be sent up to parliament, for a reform in parliament; then I perceived every thing that was to overthrow the constitution.
Q. How soon did you find out this?
A. I forsook it as soon as ever I found it out.

Q. When you found that they did not mean a petition to parliament, you determined to have nothing more to do with it after that?

A. No.

Q. Then how came you ever to go again, when Mr. Walker, who was at the head of it, told you before, when you went there the second time, that he would overthrow the constitution by and by?

A. I did not conceive the word; I was not absolutely up to that word; I did not know the meaning of the word, till late.

Q. So, when he asked you how the Volunteers were going on, and you told him, very well, he said, we shall overthrow the constitution by and by; what did you think he meant?

A. I did not know what he meant; I thought we might have a reform; that was what I wanted.

Q. You thought when Mr. Walker said, we shall overthrow the constitution by and by, that he meant a reform?

A. I did indeed, upon my oath.

Q. When you heard him say, that he would think no more of cutting the King's head off, than he would of tearing a piece of paper, you still thought he was perfectly friendly to the constitution?

A. A letter was read with respect to the King of France; I did not know but he might be guilty; they had every information from France.

Q. I am not talking of the King of France.

A. No, I am speaking that there were letters every night that the society met, coming from France. I thought he was perfectly right.

Q. I am not speaking of the King of France, but of our King. When you heard Mr. Walker say, that he should think no more, as you tell us, of cutting the King of England's head off, than of tearing a piece of paper, how came you to go afterwards?

A. Many things might induce me.

Q. You was always a Friend to the King and Constitution?

A. Yes I always served his Majesty, and will serve him still.

Q. And always thought, till you left the society, that they were people that meant well to government, and meant to reform?

A. Yes.

Q. You having served the King by sea and land, having fought for him, and being ready to fight for him again, how came you to go within the walls of that place, after hearing Mr. Walker make use of those expressions of him, and hearing those other persons talk in the manner you say that they did, of your own sovereign? You attended forty or fifty times after that, you say?

A. Suppose I did, perhaps I went there to learn; I don't know what I might do.

Q. After you had been present and heard, according to your own account, abominable treason against the chief magistrate of the country, your own gracious Sovereign, you went there to learn, did you? Now when you heard Mr. Yorke say he was going through the three kingdoms, to know what force could be collected among the different societies, to bring in the French, and to aid them, if the French landed, how came you to go to this place as a lover of your King and country?

A. I own myself in a fault to attend them?

Q. You said just now, you thought at first going off they were good people, and you never left them till you found the contrary; now did you leave them, did you voluntarily go and give any information about what you knew in this place, or did you not continue with the society as you began it, till you was taken up and put in custody?

A. I was not put in custody.

Q. Was you taken up?

A. Yes.

Q. You was arrested?

A. Yes.

Q. Did you ever open your mouth, friend as you was to your King, and a lover of your country, after you heard these people damning the King every night for months, that the chairman stated he would go round and collect force to destroy his Majesty, and bring in the French, did you ever utter one syllable of this till you was taken up and arrested?

A. I was arrested, but not put in custody.

Q. Was you not carried before a magistrate?

A. I was; I will acknowledge every thing that is lawful and just.

Q. So, all this time you was a perfect good friend to your King and country?

A. I had an opinion quite different a long time before.

Q. In what?

A. Against what I saw; I did not like the French; I think if they were to come here, if we had the same as they are getting in France, we should be very bad.

Q. So we all think; so you always did?

A. I did not always; not for some little time, a very little time.

Q. I suppose you stayed in the society a great while after you saw all this?

A. No, I did not; there was one or another hanging after me to belong to the society.

Q. Did you not stay in the society, and attend the meetings, till you was taken up for distributing a paper?

A. It was a considerable time before that.

Q. Had you never given an account of any thing you are giving to-day, till after you was taken up and carried before a magistrate?

A. No.

Q. You was never in prison?

A. No, never in my life.

Q. Nor threatened to be imprisoned?

A. No.

Q. What was you taken up for?—was not you threatened to be imprisoned for distributing a hand-bill, and was not you actually in custody?

A. What kind of hand-bill?

E

Q. No matter what kind of hand-bill; were you not taken up and carried before Mr. Griffith?
A. Yes.
Q. Do you mean to say you was never in prison upon that?
A. No, he gave me any liberty I chose.
Q. Allowed you to go where you pleased?
A. Yes.
Q. Then you never was committed, was you?
A. No.
Q. Was not you in the New Bailey?
A. Yes.
Q. How long?
A. A considerable time.
Q. And yet not a prisoner?
A. I walked in and out as I pleased.
Q. How came you to choose to be there; what was you there for?
A. I was in dread.
Q. Of what?
A. Of the opposite party; I was in doubt whether they would not destroy me.
Q. And so you walked out when you pleased?
A. Occasionally, when I saw my own opportunity.
Q. You might have gone away where you would?
A. Certainly I might.
Q. How much drink had you the day you got into prison, before you made your confession?
A. I might have some drink.
Q. Who gave it you?
A. My own pocket.
Q. It was your own money, was it?
A. Yes.
Q. Nobody else gave you any?
A. No, upon my oath; that is plump.
Q. Nobody gave you any shrub?
A. Not that day.
Q. Who gave you the shrub the next day?
A. Suppose a gentleman was so friendly as to give me a glass of shrub, is that any thing?
Q. I am not finding fault with it. Who was it?
A. I don't know whether that is to be answered or not?
Mr. *Law.* Yes, it is.
Mr. *Erskine.* I do not wish to press the gentleman.
A. I got a glass of shrub, certainly; I do not suppose that is any material matter.
Mr. Justice *Heath.* You have nothing to do whether it is material or no; answer the question.
A. I got a glass of shrub from Mr. Griffith's house, to be sure.
Q. Tell me whether I misunderstood you, or no, that you had served the King, you wish to serve him, you love him as every subject ought to love him, and that you heard all these expressions of danger to his authority mentioned in this place, then you must necessarily have thought Mr. Walker a very dangerous and wicked man from this?

A. I always thought him a good man.

Q. Not after that, did you?

A. Yes.

Q. What! after you heard him say that he would think no more of breaking the oath which he had sworn to the King, that you think him a good man after that; then you think him a good man now, perhaps?

A. I hope there may be a reformation in him.

Q. You thought him then, no doubt, and think now, that he is a very wicked man; but you hope, as every good man should, that there may be a reformation in him?

That is my hope.

A. Have you always been of that way of thinking; it is your wish he should reform; you are conscious of his wickedness; is that so? You know, if that be true, you have done nothing more than your duty to God and your country, in the oath you have taken to-day, and the oath you took before the Grand Jury, you know that?

A. I know that very well.

Q. You know you are bound to do it by every thing that is sacred; if that be so, give me leave to ask you how you came to be desirous of asking pardon of Mr. Walker for having wronged him, for having sworn falsely against him, believing him to be what you tell my Lord and these Gentlemen now: you never perhaps asked him pardon for the oath you took before the Grand Jury?

A. Never in my life.

Q. You never went down upon your knees before him, and begged for his forgiveness for the crimes which you had committed to his prejudice?

A. Never; nor I never will.

Q. You never said, did you, that you could never sleep until you had done him justice, and that you was determined to go that night to find him out?

No, never in my life.

Q. Then, of course, it is not true, that you went down upon your knees, that you wept, and held your hands before your face, when you confessed the perjury that you had committed?

A. I don't know what you may say; you may say just as you please.

Q. It is all a falsehood, and an invention of mine. I came down here to insult you, and am keeping my word.

A. Yes.

Q. You never said that Mr. Walker never had been guilty of any of those crimes that you had imputed to him?

A. No, I never did.

Q. It is entirely false?

A. I allow it to be false, the greatest falsehood that ever was expressed in a court.

Q. Have I understood you right, that three of them had damned the King, at the early parts of the meeting, Mr. Paul, Mr. Walker, and Mr. Jackson?

A. I do not recollect.

Q. Then do you not recollect that Mr. Jackson or Mr. Paul damn'd the King?

A. Yes, I do very well.
Q. Mr. Collier damn'd the King?
A. Yes.
Q. Let us hear what he said. Collier is a good deal given to swearing, is not he?
A. I never heard him in my life swear before that?
Q. What did he say?
A. He came in, and walked round, and said, he is guillotined; damn him, and all kings! I wish they were all guillotined; I wish they were all served so, he said.

Thomas Dunn.

Re-examined by Mr. *Wood.*

Q. Was you introduced to Mr. Walker and his brother at any time lately?
A. Yes, I was.
Q. When was that?
A. It was, I think, a fortnight this day.
Q. Who was it that brought you to them?
A. One Twifs.
Q. Who is he?
A. He lives close by him.
Q. Is he a servant of Mr. Walker?
A. He works for him I think.
Q. When you was brought there to Mr. Walker, what did they say to you?
A. They did not say a great deal, only two or three words passed; Richard Walker said he wondered I should deviate from my former principles, what he had taken me to be.
Q. Was there only Thomas Walker there, and Richard Walker, and Twifs?
A. I do not recollect any more. There were some words in the indictment, he said, that were not right, and I corrected them the next day.
Q. You mean the information, I suppose.
Mr. Serjeant *Cockell.* What has Richard Walker to do with Mr. Thomas Walker?
Mr. *Wood.* Was Mr. Thomas Walker there?
A. He was.
Mr. *Erskine.* I have no objection to your asking him any thing about Richard Walker.
Q. Did you never go by the name of Litchfield?
A. No, never.
Q. Where were these arms placed?
A. In the warehouse.
Mr. *Wood.* How high was the warehouse?
A. Three or four stories high.
Q. At a considerable height?

A. Yes.
Q. Could they shoulder their arms in it?
A. Yes.
Mr. *Erskine.* Pretty near as high as this place?
A. Not quite.

Thomas Kinnaston (sworn.)

Examined by Mr. *Topping.*

Q. You are, I believe, the deputy-constable of Salford?
A. Yes.
Q. And have been so some time?
A. Some years.
Q. Do you remember at any time in the months of January and February last, watching about the house of Mr. Thomas Walker?
A. Yes, in the months of January and February 1793, I did.
Q. You watched as a constable, for the purpose of seeing who went in and out there?
A. I did.
Q. At what time of the night have you used to watch there?
A. I went a little after six, and generally stayed till nine.
Q. Did you watch repeatedly during these months?
A. Yes, I went frequently, once or twice a week.
Q. Upon the nights that you have used to watch there, once or twice a week, who have you seen go into Mr. Walker's house?
A. I saw a great number that I did not know. I saw the late witness, Dunn, go in.
Q. Have you seen M'Callum, go in?
A. Yes.
Q. Did you know John Smith?
A. No.
Q. Do you know William Paul?
A. Yes, well.
Q. Have you seen him go in?
A. Yes.
Q. Have you seen Samuel Jackson?
A. Yes.
Q. Cheetham?
A. Yes.
Q. Oliver Pearsall?
A. Yes, I did not know him at that time; I have since known his name.
Q. Benjamin Booth?
A. Yes.
Q. Did you know Henry Yorke.
A. No.
Q. Do you know Dr. Collier?
A. He lives next door to Mr. Walker.

Q. You don't recollect whether you have seen him or not?
A. No.
Q. Have you seen these people repeatedly go into Mr. Walker's upon the nights you have been watching?
A. I have, some of them many times.
Q. Which door had they used to go in at?
A. At the front door.
Q. Have you seen them come out?
A. Yes, I have seen them come out.
Q. How had they used to come out?
A. At the same door.
Q. How were they admitted?
A. A very gentle tap at the door; there appeared to me to be a servant attending at the door, who seemed to know their faces perfectly well.
Q. How long had they used to remain there?
A. From the time I saw them go in, to the time of their coming out, has been more than two hours; they sometimes came out and went in again.
Q. And sometimes stayed a longer, sometimes a shorter time, I suppose?
A. Yes.
Q. Have you seen various other persons besides the persons you mentioned, go there?
A. I saw a great number of persons whom I did not know.
Q. How many in number do you think you have seen go in of an evening?
A. I believe I have seen more than fifty.
Q. Were these tradesmen of the town that you were acquainted with, or of the lower class of people?
A. A great majority seemed to be of the lower class of people; they appeared to me a great majority to be mechanics of the lower order.
Q. Did you never see them come in or go out at any door but at the front door?
A. I have seen people come out, but they might be his servants out of the warehouse, come out of the back door.
Q. You have seen people come out at the back door?
A. I have, but they might be Mr. Walker's servants for aught I know.

Thomas Kinnaston.

Cross-examined by Mr. Serjeant *Cockell.*

Q. Did you ever knock at the door?
A. I never did.
Q. Where might you stand at this time—you are rather hard of hearing?
A. I am.
Q. How did you hear this very gentle tap?

A. I was not deaf then.

Q. Was you close to the door?

A. There was a wall close to the door; I leaned against that wall frequently.

Q. Did you know the persons of these men—had you seen them before?

A. Yes, many times.

Q. Where had you seen them before?

A. Frequently in the streets.

Q. Don't you know they had their clubs at public houses, and till they got a room, it was held at Mr. Walker's?

A. I never saw them at the public-houses; I believe I should not have been admitted.

Q. Were those persons that you saw go into Mr. Walker's house, members of the club?

A. I believe they were.

Q. They were prevented holding the clubs at the public-houses?

A. I do not know that.

Q. You must know that?

A. No, I was not present.

Q. Have you not seen the public advertisements appearing in the papers?

A. I have.

Q. Do not you know that these clubs were transferred to Mr. Walker's house, till they could find some place at which to meet?

A. I do not upon my word; I know the landlords signed their names in the public papers, that they would not admit such clubs, but I know nothing of the adjournments.

Q. Do not you know, that after the landlords had so refused to receive them, at the desire of the magistrates, that they met at a private house, which was attacked by a mob and in a great measure destroyed?

A. No, I do not.

Thomas Kinnaston.

Re-examined by Mr. *Topping.*

Q. You had not an opportunity, from the situation in which you was out of doors, of observing any thing that was going on above stairs?

A. No; Mr. Walker's warehouse windows are in the yard at the back part of the house.

End of the Evidence for the Crown.

Mr. *Erskine*.

Gentlemen of the Jury,

I listened with the greatest attention (and in honour of my learned friend I must say with the greatest approbation) to much of his address to you in the opening of this Cause; it was candid and manly, and contained many truths which I have no interest to deny; one in particular which involves in it indeed the very principle of the defence, the value of that happy constitution of government, which has so long existed in this island: I hope in God that none of us will ever forget the gratitude which we owe to the Divine Providence, and, under its blessing, to the wisdom of our forefathers, for the happy establishment of law and justice under which we live; and under which, thank God, my clients are this day to be judged: great indeed will be the condemnation of any man who does not feel and act as he ought to do upon this subject; for surely if there be one privilege greater than another which the benevolent Author of our beings has been pleased to dispense to his creatures since the existence of the earth which we inhabit, it is to have cast our lots in such a country and such an age as that in which we live: for myself, I would in spirit prostrate myself daily and hourly before heaven to acknowledge it, and instead of coming from the the house of Mr. Walker, and accompanying him at Preston, (the only truths which the witness has uttered since he came into court) if I believed him capable of committing the crimes he is charged with, I would rather have gone into my grave than have been found as a friend under his roof.

Gentlemen, the crime imputed to the defendants is a serious one indeed;—Mr. Law has told you, and told you truly, that this indictment has not at all for its object to condemn or to question the particular opinions which Mr. Walker and the other defendants may entertain concerning the principles of this government or the reforms which the wisest governments may from time to time require: he is indeed a man of too enlarged a mind to think for a moment that his country can be served by interrupting the current of liberal opinion, or overawing the legal freedom of English sentiment by the terrors of criminal prosecution: he openly disavows such a system, and has, I think, even more than hinted to us that there may be seasons when an attention to reform may be salutary, and that every individual under our happy establishment has a right upon this important subject to think for himself.

The defendants therefore are not arraigned before you, nor even censured in observation, for having associated at Manchester to promote what they felt to be the cause of religious and civil liberty; nor are they arraigned or censured for seeking to collect the sentiments of their neighbours and the public concerning the necessity of a reform in the constitution of parliament; these sentiments and objects are wholly out of the question: but they are charged with having unlawfully confederated and conspired to destroy and overthrow the government of the kingdom by OPEN FORCE AND REBELLION, and that to effect this wicked purpose they exercised the King's subjects with arms, perverting that which is our birth-right for the protection of our lives and property to the malignant purpose of supporting the enemies of this kingdom in case of an invasion; in order, as my friend has truly said, for I admit the consequence if the fact is established, in order to make our country that scene of confusion and desolation which fills every man's heart with dismay and horror when he only reads or thinks of what is transacting at a distance upon the bloody theatre of the war that now reigns in the world. This, and nothing different or less than this, is the charge which is made upon the defendants, at the head of whom stands before you a merchant of honour, property, character and respect; who has long enjoyed the countenance and friendship of many of the worthiest and most illustrious persons in the kingdom, and whose principles and conduct have more than once been publicly and gratefully acknowledged by the community of which he is a member, for standing forth the friend of their commerce and liberties and the protector of the most essential privileges which Englishmen can enjoy under the laws.

Gentlemen, such a prosecution against such a person ought to have had a strong foundation; and, indeed, putting private justice and all respect of persons wholly out of the question, should not, but upon the most clear conviction and the most urgent necessity, have been instituted at all: we are at this moment in a most awful and fearful crisis of affairs; we are told authentically by the sovereign from the throne that our enemies in France are meditating an invasion, and the kingdom from one end to another is putting in motion to repel it:—in such a state of things, and when the public transactions of government and justice in the two countries pass and repass from one another as if upon the wings of the wind, is it a politic thing to prepare this solemn array of justice upon such a dangerous subject without a reasonable foundation, or rather without an urgent call, and at a time too when it is our common interest that France should believe us to be what we are and ever have been, one heart and soul to protect our country and our constitution?—Is it wise or prudent, putting private justice wholly out of the question, that it should appear to the councils of France, apt enough to exaggerate advantages, that the judge representing the government in the northern district of this kingdom should be sitting here in judgment in the presence of all the gentlemen whose property lies in the country, assembled, I observe, upon the occasion, and very properly, to witness so interesting a process, to trace and to punish the existence of a rebellious conspiracy to support an invasion from France? A conspiracy not existing in a single district alone, but maintaining itself by criminal concert and correspondence in every district, town, and city in the kingdom; projecting nothing less than the utter destruction and subversion of all the authorities of the country: Good God! can it be for the interest of government that such a state of this country should go forth?—Unfortunately the rumour and effect of this day's business will spread where the evidence may not travel with it to serve as an antidote to the mischief; for, certainly it never will nor can be

F

believed in France, or in Europe, who know the spirit of our laws, what we are witnesses to to-day;—it never will be credited that all this serious process has no foundation either in fact or probability, and that it stands upon the single evidence of a common soldier, or rather a common vagabond, discharged as unfit to be a soldier; a wretch, lost to every sense of God and religion, who avows, that he has none for either, and who is incapable of observing even common decency as a witness in the court: this will never be believed, and the country, whose best strength at home and abroad is the opinion and confidence of soundness in all its members, will suffer from the credit which government will receive for the justice of this proceeding.

What then can be more beneficial than that you should make haste as public and private men to undeceive the world, to do justice to your fellow subjects, and vindicate your country:—what can be more beneficial than that you, as honest men, should upon your oaths pronounce and record by your verdict, that however Englishmen may differ in religious opinions, which in such a land of thinking ever must be the case; that however they may separate in political speculations as to the wisest and best formation of a house of commons; that though some may think highly of the church and its establishment, whilst others, but with equal sincerity, prefer the worship of God with other ceremonies, or without any ceremonies; that though some may think that it is unsafe to touch the constitution at this particular moment, and some that at no time it is safe to touch it, while others think that its very existence depends upon immediate reformation, and that this is of all seasons the wisest for men of rank and property, while yet they have authority and influence, to employ these high trusts of high station for the universal good; what can be more beneficial than that your verdict should establish that though the country is thus divided upon these political subjects, as it ever has been in every age and period of our history, yet that we all recollect that we live in the land which our fathers have left us as an inheritance, that we all know and feel we have one common duty and one common interest, and that we are all ready to stand or fall by our country: this will be the language of your verdict whatever you yourselves may think upon these topics connected with, but still collateral to the cause: —whether you shall approve or disapprove of the opinions or objects of the defendants. I know that you will still with one mind revolt with indignation at the evidence you have heard, when you shall have heard also the observations I have to make upon it, and, what is far more important, the facts I shall bring forward to encounter it; to these last words I beg your particular attention: I say when you shall hear *the facts with which I mean to encounter the evidence*, because my learned friend has supposed that I had nothing with which to support the cause, but by railing at his witness and endeavouring to traduce his character by calling others to reproach it: he has said that I could encounter his testimony by *no one fact*, but that he had only to apprehend the influence which my address might have upon you; as if I, an utter stranger here, could have any possible weight or influence, to oppose to him who has been so long known and honoured in this place.

But although my learned friend seems to have expected no adverse evidence, he appears to have been apprehensive for the credit and consistency of his own; for he has told you that we have drawn this man into a lure not uncommon for the purpose of entrapping witnesses into a contradiction of testimony; that we have ensnared him into the company of persons who have drawn him in by insidious questions, and written down what he has been made to declare to them in destruction of his original evidence, for the wicked purpose of attacking the sworn testimony of truth and cutting down the consequences which would have followed from it to the defendants. If such a scene of wickedness has been practised it must be known to the witness himself, yet my learned friend will recollect that though he made this charge in his hearing before his examination, he has positively denied the whole of it; for I put it to him point by point, pursuing the opening as my guide: the witness denies that he has been drawn into any lure; he denies that any trap has been laid for him; he denies that he has been asked any questions by any body;—if I am mistaken I desire to be corrected, and particularly so by my learned friend, because I wish to state it as it is;—he has then denied all these things; he has further sworn that he never acknowledged to Mr. Walker that he had wronged or injured him, or that the evidence he had given against him was false; that he never had gone down upon his knees in his presence, to implore his forgiveness; that he never held his hands before his face to hide the tears that were flowing down his face in the moment of contrition, or of terror at the consequence of his crimes: all this he has positively and repeatedly sworn in answer to questions deliberately put to him; and instead of answering with doubt or as trying to recollect whether any thing approaching such a representation had happened, he put his hands to his sides and laughed, as you saw, at me who put the questions, with that sneer of contempt and insolence which has accompanied the whole of his evidence, on my part at least of his examination:—if nothing therefore was at stake but the destruction of this man's evidence and with it the prosecution which rests for its whole existence upon it, I should proceed at once to confound him with testimony, the truth of which my learned friend himself, will I am sure not bring into question; but as I wish the whole conduct of my clients to stand fairly before you and not to rest merely upon positive swearing destructive of positive testimony, and as I wish the evidence I mean to bring before you and the falsehood of that which it opposes to be clearly understood, I will state to you how it has happened that this strange prosecution has come before you.

The town of Manchester has been long extremely divided in religious and civil opinions, and while I wish to vindicate those whom I represent in this place I desire not to inflame differences which I hope in a short season will be forgotten; I wish on the contrary that every thing which proceeds from me may be the means of conciliating rather than exasperating dissentions which have already produced much mischief, and which perhaps but for the lesson of to-day might have produced much more.

Gentlemen, you all know that there have been for centuries past in this country various sects of Christians worshipping God in different forms, and holding a diversity of religious opinions; and that the law has for a long season deprived numerous classes, even of his Majesty's protestant subjects, of privileges which it confers upon the rest of the public, setting as it were a mark upon them and keeping them below the level of the community, by shutting them out from offices of trust and confidence in the country: whether these laws be wise or unwise, whether they ought to be continued or abolished, are questions for the legislature and not for us; but thus much I am warranted in saying, that it is the undoubted privilege of every man or class of men in England, to petition parliament for the removal of any system or law, which either actually does aggrieve or which is thought to be a grievance: impressed with the sense of this inherent privilege this very Constitutional Society, which is supposed by my learned friend the attorney general to have started upon the breaking out of the war with France, for the purpose of destroying the constitution, this very society owed its birth to the assertion of this indisputable birth right of Englishmen, which the authors of this prosecution most rashly thought proper to stigmatize and resist. It is well known that in 1790 the Dissenters in the different parts of the kingdom were solicitous to bring before parliament their application to put an end for ever to all divisions upon religious subjects, and to make us all, what I look forward yet to see us, one harmonious body, living like one family together; it is also well remembered with what zeal and eloquence that great question was managed in the House of Commons by Mr. Fox; and the large majority with which the repeal of the Test Acts was rejected; it seems therefore strange that the period of this rejection should be considered as an æra either of danger to the church or of religious triumph to Christians; nevertheless, a large body of gentlemen and others at Manchester, whose motives I am far from wishing to scrutinize or condemn, considered this very wish of the Dissenters as injurious to their rights, and as dangerous to the church and state; they published advertisements expressive of these sentiments, and the rejection of the bill in the commons produced a society stiled the Church and King Club, which met for the first time to celebrate what they called the glorious decision of the House of Commons in rejecting the prayer of their dissenting brethren.

Gentlemen, it is not for me to say, that it was unjust or impolitic in parliament to reject the application; but surely I may without offence suggest, that it was hardly a fit subject of triumph that a great number of fellow-subjects, amounting I believe to more than a million in this country, had miscarried in an object which they thought beneficial, and which they had a most unquestionable right to submit to the government under which they lived; yet for this cause alone, (France and every other topic of controversy being yet unborn,) was the Church and King held forth to be in danger: a society instituted for their protection, and an uniform appointed with the church of Manchester upon its button.

Gentlemen, without calling for any censure upon this proceeding, but leaving it to every man's own reflection, is it to be wondered at or condemned, that those who thought more largely and liberally on subjects of freedom both civil and religious, but who found themselves perfecuted for fentiments and conduct, the moft avowedly legal and conftitutional, fhould affociate for the fupport of their rights and privileges as Englifhmen, and affemble to confider how they might beft obtain a more adequate reprefentation of the people of Great Britain in parliament.

Gentlemen, this fociety continued with thefe objects in view until the iffuing of the proclamation againft Republicans and Levellers, calling upon the magiftrates to exert themfelves throughout the kingdom to avert fome danger with which it feems our rulers thought this kingdom was likely to be vifited; of this danger or the probability of it either *generally* or at Manchefter in *particular* my learned friend has given no evidence from any quarter but that of Mr. Dunn; he has not proved that there has been in any one part of the kingdom any thing which could lead government to apprehend that meetings exifted for the purpofes pointed at; but that is out of the queftion; government had a right to think for itfelf and to iffue the proclamation; the publicans however, (as it appears upon the crofs examination of the witnefs,) probably directed by the migiftrates, thought fit to fhut up their houfes opened by immemorial law to all the King's fubjects, and to refufe admiffion to all the gentlemen and tradefmen of the town who did not affociate under the banners of this Church and King Club: this illegal proceeding was accompanied with an advertifement containing a vehement libel againft all thofe perfons who under the protection of the laws thought themfelves as much at liberty to confider their various privileges, as others were to maintain the eftablifhment of the church. Upon this occafion Mr. Walker honourably ftood forth, opened his houfe to this Conftitutional Society at a time when they muft otherwife have been in the ftreets by a combination of the publicans to reject them. Now, Gentlemen, I put it to you as men of honour, whether it can be juftly attributed to Mr. Walker as feditious or hoftile to the liberties of his country, that he opened his houfe to a fociety of Gentlemen and tradefmen, whofe good principles he was acquainted with, who had been wantonly oppofed by this Church and King Club, whofe privileges they had never invaded or queftioned, and againft whom, in this day of trial, there is no man to be found who can come forward to impeach an act they have done, or a fyllable they have uttered: vehement as the defire moft apparently has been to bring this Gentleman and his affociates as they are called to juftice, yet not one magiftrate, no man of property, part or figure in this town or its neighbourhood, no perfon having the King's authority in Manchefter or the county, have appeared to prove one fact or circumftance from whence even the vagueft fufpicion could arife, that any thing criminal had been intended or tranfacted: no conftable who had ever been fent to guard left the peace might be broken or to make enquiries for its prefervation; not a paper feized throughout England, nor any other profecution inftituted except upon the evidence of the fame miferable wretch who ftands before you, but the town, neighbourhood, and county, were in the fame profound ftate of tranquillity as they are at the moment I am addreffing you.

Gentlemen, at the time parliament affembled at the end of 1792, previous to the commencement of the war, thefe unhappy differences were fuddenly (and as you will fee from no fault of Mr. Walker) brought to the crifis which produced this trial: a meeting was held in Manchefter to prepare an addrefs of thanks to the King for having embodied the militia during the recefs of parliament, and for having put the kingdom into a pofture of defence; and I do not feek to queftion the meafure of government which gave rife to this approbation or the approbation itfelf which they had a right to beftow; but others had an equal right to entertain other opinions; on all public meafures the decifion undoubtedly is with government, but the people at the fame time have a right to think upon them and to exprefs what they think;—furely war of all other fubjects is one which the people have a right to confider; furely it can be no offence for thofe whofe properties were to be taxed and whofe inheritances were to be leffened by it, to paufe a little upon the eve of a conteft, the end of which no man can forefee, the expences of which no man can calculate, nor eftimate the blood to flow from its calamities; furely it is a liberty fecured to us by the firft principles of our conftitution to addrefs the Sovereign, or inftruct our reprefentatives, to avert the greateft evil that can impend over a nation.

Gentlemen, one of thofe focieties called the Reformation Society met to exercife this undoubted privilege, and in my mind upon the fitteft occafion that ever prefented itfelf; yet mark the moderation of Mr. Walker, whofe violence is arraigned before you: though he was no member of that body, and though he agreed in the propriety of the meafure in agitation, yet he went to their meeting, fuggefted to them that their oppofition might be made a pretence for tumult, that tranquillity in fuch a crifis was by every means to be promoted, and therefore advifed them to abftain from the meeting: fo that the other meeting was left to carry their approbation of government and the war, without a diffenting voice: if ever therefore there was a time when the Church and King might be faid to be out of danger at Manchefter, it was at this moment; yet *on this very day* they hoifted the banners of alarm to both, they paraded with them through every quarter of the town; mobs by degrees were collected, and in the evening of this very eleventh of December Mr. Walker's houfe and others were attacked; you will obferve that before this day no man has talked about arms at Mr. Walker's:—if an honourable gentleman upon the Jury who has been carefully taking notes of the evidence will have the goodnefs to refer to them, he will find that it was not till near a week after this, (fo Dunn expreffes it,) that a fingle firelock had been feen, nor indeed does any part of the evidence go back beyond this time, when Mr. Walker's houfe was thus furrounded and attacked by a riotous and diforderly mob. He was aware of the probable confequences of fuch an attack, he knew by the recent example of Birmingham what he and others profeffing fentiments of freedom had to expect; he therefore got together a few fire-arms, which he had long had publicly by him, and an inventory of which with the reft of his furniture at Barlow-Hall had been taken by a fworn appraifer, long before any thing connected with this indictment had an existence; with thefe, and the affiftance of a few fteady friends, he ftood upon his defence; he was advifed indeed to retire for fafety, but knowing his own innocence, and recollecting the duty he owed to himfelf, his family and the public, he declared he would remain there to fupport the laws and to defend his property; and that he would perifh rather than furrender thofe privileges which every member of the community is bound both from intereft and duty to maintain:—to alarm the multitude he fired from the windows over their heads, and difperfed them: the next morning they affembled in very great numbers before his houfe, when a man got upon the church-yard wall, and read a moft violent and inflammatory paper, and harangued and incited the populace to pull the houfe down; Mr. Walker went out amongft them, and expoftulated with them, and afked why they had difgraced themfelves fo much by attacking him the night before, adding that if he had done any of them or any perfon whom they knew any injury, he was, upon proof of it, ready to make them every fatisfaction in his power—he alfo told them, that he had fired upon them the night before becaufe they were mad as well as drunk, that if they attacked him again, he would under the fame circumftances act, as he had before done, but that he was then alone and unarmed in the midft of them, and if he had done any thing wrong they were then fober and had him completely in their power.

Gentlemen, this was moft meritorious conduct. You all live at a diftance from the metropolis and were probably therefore fortunate enough neither to be within or near it in 1780, when from beginnings fmaller than thofe which exhibited themfelves at Birmingham, or even at Manchefter, the metropolis of the country, and with it the country itfelf, had nearly been undone; the beginning of thefe things is the feafon for exertion: I fhall never indeed forget what I have heard the late mild and venerable magiftrate Lord Mansfield fay upon this fubject, whofe houfe was one of the firft attacked in London; I have more than once heard him fay, that perhaps fome blame might have attached upon himfelf and others in authority, for their forbearance in not having directed force to have been *at the firft moment* repelled by force, it being the higheft humanity as a check in the infancy of tumults.

Gentlemen, Mr. Walker's conduct had the defired effect: he watched again on the 13th of December, but the mob returned no more, and next morning the arms were locked up in a bed chamber in his houfe where they have remained ever fince, and where of courfe they never could have been feen by the witnefs whofe whole evidence commences above a week fubfequent to the 11th of December, when they were finally put afide.

Gentlemen, this is the genuine hiftory of the bufinefs, and it muft therefore not a little furprize you that when the charge is wholly confined to the ufe of arms, Mr. Law fhould not even have hinted to you that Mr. Walker's houfe had been attacked, and that he was driven to ftand upon his defence; as if fuch a thing had never had an exiftence; indeed the armoury which muft have been exhibited in fuch a ftatement would have but ill fuited the indictment or the evidence, and *I* must therefore undertake the description of it myself.

The arms having been locked up as I told you in the bed-chamber, I was shewn last week into this house of conspiracy, treason, and death, and saw exposed to view the mighty armoury which was to level the beautiful fabric of our constitution, and to destroy the lives and properties of seven millions of people; it consisted first of six little swivels purchased more than five years ago at the sale of Livesey, Hargrave, and Co. (of whom we have all heard so much) by Mr. Jackson a gentleman of Manchester, who is also one of the defendants, and who gave them to Master Walker, a boy about ten years of age; swivels you know are guns so called because they turn upon a pivot, but these were taken off their props, were painted, and put upon blocks resembling carriages of heavy cannon and in that shape may be fairly called children's toys; you frequently see them in the neighbourhood of London adorning the houses of sober citizens, who, strangers to Mr. Brown and his improvements, and preferring grandeur to taste, place them upon their ramparts at Mile-End or Islington: having been, like Mr. Dunn, (I hope I resemble him in nothing else) having like him served his Majesty as a soldier (and I am ready to serve again if my country's safety should require it) I took a closer review of all I saw, and observing that the muzzle of one of them was broke off, I was curious to know how far this famous conspiracy had proceeded and whether they had come into action, when I found the accident had happened on firing a *feu de joie* upon his Majesty's happy recovery, and that they had been afterwards fired upon the Prince of Wales' birth day. These are the only times that in the hands of these conspirators, these cannon big with destruction had opened their little mouths; once to commemorate the indulgent and benign favour of Providence in the recovery of the Sovereign, and once as a congratulation to the Heir apparent of his crown on the anniversary of his birth.

I went next, under the protection of the master-general of this ordnance (Mr. Walker's chambermaid,) to visit the rest of this formidable array of death, and found next a little musketoon about so high, *(describing it,)* I put my thumb upon it, when out started a little bayonet like the Jack-in-a-box which we buy for children at a fair; In short, not to weary you gentlemen, there was just such a parcel of arms of different sorts and sizes as a man collecting amongst his friends, for his defence against the sudden violence of a riotous multitude, might be expected to have collected; here lay three or four rusty guns of different dimensions, and here and there a bayonet or broad sword covered over with dust so as to be almost undistinguishable; for notwithstanding what this infamous wretch has sworn, we will prove by witness after witness, till you desire us to finish, that they were principally collected on the 11th of December, the day of the riot, and that from the 12th in the evening, or the 13th in the morning, they have been untouched as I have described them; that their use began and ended with the necessity, and that from that time to the present there never has been a fire-arm in the warehouse of any sort or description; this is the whole on which has been built a proceeding which might have brought the defendants to the punishment of death, for both the charge and the evidence amount to high treason, high treason indeed under almost every branch of the statute; for the facts amount to levying war against the King by a conspiracy to wrest by force the government out of his hands; to an adherence to the King's enemies, and to a compassing of his death, which is a necessary consequence of an invading army of republicans or of any other enemies of the state; yet notwithstanding the notoriety of these facts, the unnamed prosecutors (and indeed I am afraid to slander any man or body of men by even a guess upon the subject,) have been beating up as for volunteers, to procure another witness to destroy the lives of the gentlemen before you, against many of whom warrants for high treason were issued to apprehend them; Mr. Walker among the rest was the subject of such a warrant, and as soon as he knew it, he behaved (as he has throughout) like a man and an Englishman: he wrote immediately to the Secretary of State who was summoned here to day, and whose absence I do not complain of, because we have by consent the benefit of his testimony; he wrote three letters to Mr. Dundas, one of which was delivered by Mr. Wharton, informing him that he was in London on his business as a merchant; that if any warrant had been issued against him he was ready to meet it, and for that purpose delivered his address where it might be executed*: this Mr. Walker did when the prosecutors were in search of another witness, and when this Mr. Dunn was walking like a tame sparrow through the New Bailey, fed at the public or some other expence, and suffered to go at large, though arrested upon a criminal charge and sent into custody under it.

And to what other circumstances need I appeal for the purity of the defendants, than that under the charge of a conspiracy extensive enough to comprehend in its transactions (if any existed) the whole compass of England, the tour of which was to have been made by Mr. Yorke, there has not been one man found to utter a syllable about them, no not one man, thanks be to God, who has so framed the characteristics of Englishmen, except the solitary infamous witness before you, who from what I have heard since I began to address you, may have spoken the truth when he claimed my acquaintance, as I have reason to think he has seen me before in a criminal court of justice.

Having now for the satisfaction of the defendants rather than from the necessity of the case, given you an account of their whole proceedings as I shall establish them by proof, let us now examine the evidence that has been given against them, and see how the truth of it could stand with reason or probability, supposing it to have been sworn to by a witness the most respectable.

According to Dunn's own account, Mr. Walker had not been at the first meeting, so that when he first saw Dunn he did not know either his person or his name, he might have been a spy (God knows there are enow of them) and at that season in particular, inform-

---

* See Appendix, No. i. to xi.

ers were to be expected, Mr. Walker is supposed to have said to him, "What is your business here?" to which he answered, "I am going to the society," which entitled him at once to admission without further ceremony; there was nobody to stop him, was he asked his name? was he balloted for? was he questioned as to his principles? No, he walked in at once, but first it seems Mr. Walker, who had never before seen him, enquired of him the news from Ireland, (observing by his voice that he was an Irishman) and asked what the Volunteers were about, as if Mr. Walker could possibly suppose that such a person was likely to have been in a correspondence with Ireland which told him more than report must have told every body else; Mr. Dunn tells you indeed he was no such person, he was a friend, as he says, to the King and Constitution which Mr. Walker would have found by asking another question, but without further enquiry he is supposed to have said to him at once, "we shall overthrow the constitution by and by," which the moment Dunn had heard, up walked that affectionate subject of our Sovereign Lord the King into Mr. Walker's house where the constitution was to be so overthrown; but then he tells you he thought there was no harm to be done, that it was only for the benefit of the poor, and the public good; but how could he think so after what he had that moment heard? but he did not know it seems what Mr. Walker meant. Gentlemen, do you collect from Mr. Dunn's discourse and deportment to day that he could not tell but that a man meant good when he had heard him even express *a wish* to overthrow the government; would you pull a feather out of a sparrow's wing upon the oath of a man who swears that he believed a person to have been a good subject in the very moment he was telling him of an intended rebellion? But why should I fight a phantom with argument? Could any man but a driveller, have possibly given such an answer as is put into Mr. Walker's mouth to a man he had never seen in his life? However many may differ from Mr. Walker in opinion, every body I believe will admit that he is an acute, intelligent man, with an extensive knowledge of the world, and not at all likely to have conducted himself like an idiot: what follows next?—another night he went into the warehouse where he saw Mr. Yorke called to the chair, who said he was going the tour of the kingdom in order to try the strength of the different societies to join fifty thousand men that were expected to land from France into this country, and that Mr. Walker then said, " Damn all kings—I know our King has seventeen millions " of money in the Bank of Vienna although he won't afford any " of it to the poor." Gentlemen, is this the language of a man of sense and education? If Mr. Walker had the malignity of a demon, would he think of giving effect to it by such a senseless lie?— When we know that from the immense expence attending his Majesty's numerous and illustrious family and the great necessities of the state, he has been obliged over and over again to have recourse to the generosity and justice of parliament to maintain the dignity of the crown, could Mr. Walker ever have thought of inventing this nonsense about the Bank of Vienna, when there is a Bank too in our own country where he might legally invest his property for himself and his heirs? but Mr. Walker did not stop there; he went in and said, "I should think no more of taking off the King's head 'than I should of tearing this piece of paper." All this happened soon after Dunn's admission, yet this man who represents himself to you upon his oath this day, as having been uniformly a friend to the constitution, as far as he understood it; as having left the society as soon as he saw their mischievous inclinations, and as having *voluntarily* informed against them, I say this same friend of the constitution tells you almost in the same breath, that he continued to attend their meetings from thirty to forty times *where high treason was committing with open doors*, and that instead of giving information of his own free choice, he was arrested in the very act of distributing some seditious publication.

Gentlemen, it is really a serious consideration, that upon such testimony a man should even be put upon his defence in the courts of this country; upon such principles what man is safe? I was indeed but ill at-ease myself when Mr. Dunn told me he knew me better than I supposed, what security have I at this moment that he should not swear that he had met with me under some gate-way in Lancaster and that I had said to him, " Well, Dunn, I " hope you will not swear against Mr. Walker, but that you will " stick to the good cause : damn all kings : damn the constitution :" if the witness were now to swear this, into gaol I must go, and if my client is in danger from what has been sworn against *him* what safety would there be for *me?* the evidence would be equally positive, and I am equally an object of suspicion as Mr. Walker; it is said of *him* that he has been a member of a society for the reform of parliament ; so have *I*, and so am *I* at this moment, and so at all hazards I will continue to be, and I will tell you why gentlemen, because I hold it to be essential to the preservation of all the ranks and orders of the state, alike essential to the prince and to the people : I have the honour to be allied to his Majesty in blood, and my family has been for centuries a part of what is now called the aristocracy of the country, I can therefore have no interest in the destruction of the constitution.

In pursuing the probability of this story, (since it must be pursued) let us next advert to whether any thing appears to have been done in other places which might have been exposed by this man's information : the whole kingdom is under the eye and dominion of magistracy awakened at that time to an extraordinary vigilance, yet has any one man been arrested even upon the suspicion of any correspondence with the societies of Manchester, good, bad or indifferent, or has any person within the four seas come to swear that any such correspondence existed? so that you are desired to believe upon Mr. Dunn's single declaration that gentlemen of the description I am representing, without any end or object, or concert with others, were resolved to put their lives into the hands of any miscreant who might be disposed to swear them away, by holding public meetings of conspiracy with open doors and in the presence of all mankind, liable to be handed over to justice every moment of their lives, since every tap at the door might have introduced a constable as readily as a member; and, to finish the absurdity, these gentlemen are made to discourse in a manner that would difgrace the lowest and most uninformed classes of the community.

Let us next see what interest Mr. Walker has in the proposed invasion of this peaceable country: Has Mr. Law proved that Mr. Walker had any reason to expect protection from the French from any secret correspondence or communication more than you or I have, or that he had prepared any means of resisting the troops of this country? how was he to have welcomed these strangers into our land? what with this dozen of rusty muskets, or with those conspirators whom he exercised? but who are they? they are it seems " to the jurors unknown," as my learned friend has called them who drew this indictment, and he might have added *who will ever remain unknown to them;*—but has Mr. Walker nothing to lose like other men who dread an invasion? He has long had the acquaintance and friendship of some of the best men in this kingdom, who would be destroyed if such an invasion should take place—Has he like other men no ties of a nearer description? Alas, gentlemen! I feel at this moment that he has many: Mr. Dunn told you that I was with Mr. Walker at Manchester, and it enables me to say of my own knowledge that it is impossible he should have had the designs imputed to him. I have been under his roof where I have seen him the husband of an amiable and affectionate woman, and the happy parent of six engaging children; and it hurts me not a little to think what they must feel at this moment: before prosecutions are set on foot, those things ought to be considered; we ought not like the fool in the proverbs to scatter fire-brands and death, and say, " Am I not in sport?" Could we look at this moment into the dwelling of this unfortunate gentleman, for so I must call him, I am persuaded it would distress us; they cannot but be unhappy; they have seen prosecutions equally unjust as even this is, attended with a success of equal injustice, and we have seen those proceedings, I am afraid by those who are at the bottom of this indictment, put forward for your imitation. I saw to my astonishment at Preston, where as a traveller I called for a newspaper, that this immaculate society (the Manchester Church and King Club) had a meeting lately and had published to the world the toasts and sentiments which they drank; some of them I like, some of them deserve reprobation: " The Church " and King;" very well. " The Queen and Royal Family;" be it so. " The Duke of York and the army;" be it so. But what do you think came next?

(Here Mr. Justice Heath interrupted Mr. Erskine by saying we are not to go into this of which you cannot give evidence.)

Mr. *Erskine.* I don't know what effect these publications may have upon the administration of justice; why drink " *the Lord Advocate and the Court of Justiciary in Scotland,*" just when your Lordship is called upon to administer *English* justice; if I had seen the King and his judges upon the northern circuit published as a toast——

Mr. Justice *Heath.* You know you cannot give this in evidence.

Mr. *Erskine.* Gentlemen, considering the situation in which my clients stand at this moment, I expressed the idea which occurred to me and which I thought not to suppress, but let it pass; this is not the moment... controversy; it is my interest to submit to any course his Lordship may think proper to dictate; the evidence is more than enough for my purpose; so mainly improbable, so contrary to every thing in the course of human affairs, that I know you would reject it even if it stood unanswered; what then will you say when I shall prove to you by the oaths of the various persons who attended these societies, that no propositions of the sort insinuated by this witness ever existed; that no hint directly or indirectly of any illegal tendency was ever whispered; that their real objects were just what were *openly professed*, be they right or wrong, be they wise or mistaken, namely, *reformation in the constitution of the House of Commons*, which my learned friend admitted they had a right by constitutional means to promote; this was their object, they neither desired to touch the King's authority nor the existence or privileges of the House of Lords; but they wished that those numerous classes of the community who, (by the law as it now stands), are secluded from any share in the choice of members to the parliament, should have an equal right with others in concerns where their interests are equal. Gentlemen, this very county furnishes a familiar instance: there are I believe at least thirty thousand freeholders in Lancashire, each of whom has a vote for two members of parliament; and there are two boroughs within it, (if I mistake not) Clithero and Newton, containing a handful of men who are at the beck of *two individuals;* yet these two little places send for themselves, or rather for these two *persons*, two members each, which makes four against the whole power and interest of this county in parliament, touching any measure how deeply soever it may concern their prosperity: can there then be any offence in meeting together to consider of a representation to parliament, suggesting the wisdom of alteration and amendment in such a system?

Mr. Justice *Heath*. *There can be no doubt but that a petition to parliament for reform or any thing else can be no offence.*

Mr. *Erskine*. Gentlemen, I expected this interruption from the learning of the Judge; certainly it can be no offence, and consequently my clients can be no offenders.

Having now exposed the weakness of Dunn's evidence from its own intrinsic defects, and from the positive contradiction every part of it is to receive from many witnesses, I shall conclude with the still more positive and unequivocal contradiction which the whole of it has received from Dunn himself—You may remember that I repeatedly asked him whether he had not confessed that the whole he had sworn to-day was utterly false; whether he had not confessed it to be so with tears of contrition, and whether he had not kneeled down before Mr. Walker to implore his forgiveness. My learned friend knowing that this would be proved upon him, made a shrewd and artful observation to avoid the effects of it; he said that such things had fallen often under the observation of the court upon the circuit, where witnesses had been drawn into similar snares by artful people to invalidate their testimony; this may be true, but the answer to its application is, that not only the witness himself has positively denied that any such snare was number and credit will put a total end to such a suggestion; if I had indeed but one witness, my friend the Attorney General might undoubtedly put it to you in reply whether his or mine was to be believed; but I will call to you, *not one but four or five;* or, if necessary, *six witnesses* ABOVE ALL SUSPICION, in whose presence Dunn voluntarily confessed the falsehood of his testimony, and with tears of apparent repentance offered to make any reparation to these injured and unfortunate defendants; this I pledge myself to prove to your satisfaction.

Gentlemen, the object of all public trial and punishment is the security of mankind in social life; we are not assembled here for the purposes of vengeance, but for the ends of justice; to give that tranquility to human life which is the scope of all government and law; you will therefore take care how in the very administration of justice, you disappoint that which is the very foundation of its institution; you will take care that in the very moment you are trying a man as a disturber of the public happiness, you do not violate the rules which alone secure to us all our happiness as private men, to secure which we alone form a public.

The last evidence I have been stating ought by itself to put an instant end to this cause; I remember a case very lately which was so brought to its conclusion, where upon a trial for perjury of a witness who had sworn against the captain of a vessel in the African trade, it appeared that the witnesses who swore to the perjury against the defendants, had themselves made deliberate declarations which materially clashed with the testimony they were giving; Lord Kenyon, who tried the cause, would after this proceed no further, and asked me, who was of counsel for the prosecution, whether I would urge it further, saying emphatically, what I hope every Judge under similar circumstances will think it his duty to say also, " No man ought or can be convicted in England, " unless the Judge and the Jury have *a firm assurance* that inno-
" cence cannot by any possibility be the victim of conviction and " sentence." And how can the Jury or his Lordship have that assurance here, when the only source of it is brought into such serious doubt and question? Upon the whole then I cannot help hoping that my friend the Attorney General when he shall hear my proofs, will feel that a prosecution like this ought not to be offered for the seal and sanction of your verdict; *unjust prosecutions lead to the ruin of all governments; for whoever will look back to the history of the world in general, and of our own particular country, will be convinced, that exactly in proportion as prosecutions have been cruel and oppressive, and maintained by inadequate and unrighteous evidence, in the same proportion and by the same means, their authors have been destroyed instead of being supported by them; as often as the principles of our ancient laws have been departed from in weak and wicked times, as often the governments that have violated them have been suddenly crumbled into dust; and therefore wishing, as I most sincerely do, the preservation and prosperity of our happy constitution, I desire to enter my protest against its being supported by means that are likely to destroy it;* violent proceedings bring on the bitterness of retaliation until all justice and moderation are trampled down and subverted; witness

those sanguinary prosecutions previous to the awful period in the last century, when Charles the first fell: that unfortunate prince lived to lament those vindictive judgments by which his impolitic, infatuated followers imagined they were supporting his throne: he lived to see how they destroyed it; his throne, undermined by violence, sunk under him, and those who shook it were guilty in their turn; such is the natural order of injustice, not of similar but of worse and more violent wrongs; witness the fate of the unhappy Earl of Strafford, who, when he could not be reached by the ordinary laws, was impeached in the House of Commons, and who when still beyond the consequences of that judicial proceeding, was at last destroyed *by the arbitrary wicked mandate of the legislature*. James the Second lived to ask assistance in the hour of his own distress, from those whom he had cut off from the means of giving it; he lived to ask support from the Earl of Bedford after his son, the unfortunate Lord Russel, had fallen under the axe of injustice; "I once had a son," said that noble person, "who could have served your Majesty upon this occasion," but there was then none to assist him.

I cannot possibly tell how others feel upon these subjects, but I do know how it is their interest to feel concerning them; *we ought to be persuaded that the only way by which government can be honourably or safely supported, is by cultivating the love and affection of the people: by shewing them the value of the constitution by its protection; by making them understand its principles by the practical benefits derived from them, and above all, by letting them feel their security in the administration of law and justice:* what is it in the present state of that unhappy kingdom, the contagion of which fills us with such alarm, that is the just object of terror? What, but that accusation and conviction are the same, and that a false witness or power without evidence is a warrant for death? not so here;—long may the countries differ! and I am asking nothing more, than that you should decide according to our own wholesome rules, by which our government was established, and by which it has been ever protected. Put yourselves, gentlemen, in the place of the defendants, and let me ask if you were brought before your country upon a charge supported by no other evidence than that which you have heard to-day, and encountered by that which I have stated to you, what would you say, or your children after you, if you were touched in your persons or your properties by a conviction?—may you never be put to such reflections nor the country to such disgrace! The best service we can render to the public is that we should live like one harmonious family, that we should banish all animosities, jealousies, and suspicions of one another, and that living under the protection of a mild and impartial justice, we should endeavour, with one heart, according to our best judgments, to advance the freedom and maintain the security of Great Britain.

Gentlemen, I will trouble you no further; I am afraid indeed I have too long trespassed on your patience, I will therefore proceed to call my witnesses.

EVIDENCE FOR THE DEFENDANTS.

Mr. *George Wakefield* (sworn).

Examined by Mr. Serjeant *Cockell*.

Q. You are a merchant in Manchester I understand?
A. I have been.
Q. Do you remember the time of the riots when Mr. Walker's house was attacked?
A. I do.
Q. After that night do you know whether the constitutional society which had been formed in Manchester, met at Mr. Walker's?
A. Yes.
Q. Was you a member of that society?
A. I was.
Q. What was the object of that society?
A. A parliamentary reform.
Q. How happened it that after that time the meetings were held at Mr. Walker's?
A. I don't know particularly; some of the public houses had refused to let us have a room any longer.
Q. However in point of fact the meetings then were held at Mr. Walker's?
A. They were.
Q. We have heard of the time of the riots, you will speak to the day as nearly as you remember?
A. I believe it was on Tuesday the 11th of December.
Q. How often did the society meet?
A. Once a week or once a fortnight, I declare I do not recollect which.
Q. Did you ever attend those meetings?
A. Pretty regularly.
Q. How long did you continue to attend them?
A. Till nearly the last meeting I believe, which was some time in the spring of last year.
Q. Was there a free admission to any person who might choose to come?
A. Not that I know of.
Q. To members of the society?
A. There was.
Q. We have heard that men exercised with arms in the warehouse were drilled in the use of arms; is that true?
A. Not that I know of.
Q. Did you ever see such a thing?
A. No.
Q. In what part of Mr. Walker's house were the meetings held?
A. In the upper room in the warehouse.
Q. What passed at those meetings?

A. The different bufineffes refpecting the fociety.
Q. Was the King damned?
Mr. *Law.* You muſt not put that.
Mr. Serjeant *Cockell.* Tell us what was faid about the King.
A. I do not recollect hearing any thing faid about the King.
Q. Did you ever hear any thing faid about overthrowing the conſtitution by means of arms or otherwife?
A. I never heard any fuch thing.
Q. Was any thing faid about inviting the French to invade the kingdom?
A. No.
Q. Did you ever hear any thing of the fort?
A. No, not a fyllable.
Q. If men had been drilled in the ufe of fire-arms, muſt you not have feen it?
A. I muſt.
Q. Did you ever fee any?
A. No.
Q. Ever hear of any?
A. No.
Q. If any perfons had been drilled in arms for the purpofe of offence, or deſtroying the government, would you have continued a member of that fociety?
A. No, not a moment.
Q. Did you ever hear any thing faid about inviting an invafion from France?
Mr. *Law.* Aſk what did pafs there when this man was prefent.
Mr. Serjeant *Cockell.* I have no wiſh to lead.
Mr. *Erſkine.* I ſhould be forry to offer any teſtimony that is not in the ordinary courfe, but when a witnefs comes to contradict a particular point, how can we act any other way?
Mr. Juſtice *Heath.* He has faid, no mention was made of any invafion.
Mr. Serjeant *Cockell.* What was the fole object of your meeting?
A. As far as I underſtood it, a parliamentary reform.
Q. Was there any act done at your meeting to your knowledge that was directed otherwife than to that end?
A. No.
Q. Did you at any time, or any perfon in your hearing, in that room, fay or do any thing to overturn the government of the country?
A. No, never.
Q. What was the reform that you fought, and by what means?
A. That is a point upon which few people are agreed; but it was a parliamentary reform.
Q. By means of menacing government?
A. No.
Q. Inviting a foreign enemy?
A. No.
Q. Was it in any other way than fuch means as you fuppofe the law to allow?

H

A. No, by no other means than what we apprehend to be conſtitutional, nothing but what the law allows.

Mr. *Erſkine.* The witneſs has ſaid it was to be done by no other means than what in his apprehenſions the law allowed; we can go no further if we were to ſtay here a month.

Mr. Sergeant *Cockell.* You attended pretty conſtantly you have ſaid. What have you heard Mr. Walker ſay at any time?

M. Juſtice *Heath.* You may aſk him, did he hear Mr. Walker ſay any thing about the King.

Mr. Serjeant *Cockell.* What number of men might there be generally?

A. Sometimes more, and ſometimes leſs; I have ſeen twenty in the ſociety, and I have ſeen more, the numbers differing at different times.

Q. Did you ever ſee any men exerciſed in the uſe of arms?
A. No.

Q. Did you ever hear any thing of the ſort mentioned?
A. No, if I had, merely to learn the uſe of arms, I ſhould have been one myſelf probably, but I never heard any thing of it.

Q. Did you ever hear Paul or any other perſon ſay that he knew there would be a revolt from Ireland?
A. I do not recollect any ſuch thing.

Q. Did you ever hear any one ſay if we had a revolt, it would be through the Iriſh?
A. No.

Q. Did you ever hear any one ſay they had ſent a deputy to Ireland as a King, and damn him and all Kings?
A. No.

Q. Could any ſuch expreſſions have been made uſe of without your hearing of them?
A. No, I am ſure there could not.

Q. Did you ever hear Mr. Walker damn the King?
A. No.

Q. At any time?
A. No.

Q. Did you ever hear it ſaid either by Mr. Walker or any other perſon, that Mr. Yorke was going through the three kingdoms to know the aid that there might be for the French?
A. No.

Mr. *Law.* Was you there when Mr. Yorke was by?

Mr. Serjeant *Cockell.* Dunn ſaid there were every night converſations about the King.

Mr. *Walker.* Did you ever hear me ſay any thing unbecoming an honeſt man and a good citizen?

Mr. *Law.* We cannot aſk that.

Mr. Serjeant *Cockell.* Do you remember the time when Mr. Yorke was in the chair?
A. I do not recollect that I was there at that time.

Q. Did you uſe to ſkulk in privately and ſecretly?
A. No.

Q. Did you go in always the ſame way?
A. I cannot ſay whether I did at all time, I went in at different doors; I was not going about any thing I was aſhamed of.

Mr. *George Wakefield.*

Cross-examined by Mr. *Law.*

Q. You are or was a partner with **Mr.** Grant?
A. Yes.
Q. He is a brother-in-law of Mr. Walker?
A. Yes.
Q. Have you attended at most of those meetings?
A. At many of them.
Q. Did you see Dunn there at any of them?
A. I don't remember that I ever did.
Q. Not at any?
A. I believe he was not a member of the same society.
Q. Are you of the Reformation Society?
A. No; of the Constitutional Society.
Q. Did that society meet at the house of Mr. Walker?
A. Yes.
Q. They met on different nights, did they?
A. I believe so; I was not a member of any other society.
Q. Whether you saw Mr. Yorke at that meeting that you attended?
A. I do not recollect seeing him there at all.
Q. Do you know him?
A. I do not know him.
Q. How came you to have no doubt you had seen him more than once?
A. I do not recollect I said any such thing.
Q. I took you down that Yorke was by?
A. I did not say so.
Q. You don't know whether Yorke was present at any meeting?
A. I believe he was present at a meeting, but I do not recollect being there when he was.

Mr. Justice *Heath.* It was a different society.

Mr. *Erskine.* They met in the same room at the same time.

Mr. *Law.* Do you mean to say the Reformation Society and the Constitutional Society met at the same place and time under the roof of Mr. Walker?

A. Yes, occasionally; I have seen the Reformation Society there at the same time, and in the same room.

Q. As you resorted there frequently, and the societies frequently met there, if this man, Dunn, had gone to Mr. Walker's, you might probably have seen him?
A. Probably I might.
Q. Is his person familiar with you?
A. I saw him this morning.
Q. You do not recollect him?
A. I do not.

Q. What time of the year did you attend at thefe meetings?
A. Almoft all the year.
Q. From September up to June?
A. I do not recollect particularly.
Q. Do you recollect the time when Yorke was at Manchefter?
A. No.
Q. Whether you have not declared you was prefent when Mr. Yorke was at one of thefe meetings?
A. No.
Q. Have you not faid fo in this court?
A. If you have taken it down fo, you have taken it down wrong; I do not know him.
Q. Mr Thomas Walker you have feen of courfe there?
A. Yes.
Q. Mr. Cheetham?
A. Yes.
Q. Mr. Jackfon?
A. Yes.
Q. Pearfall?
A. I do not know him; I may know his perfon.
Q. M'Callum and Smith?
A. I have feen them there.
Q. Do you know where they are now?
A. No.
Q. Booth you have feen there?
A. Yes.
Q. And Paul?
A. Yes.
Q. And Collier?
A. Yes.
Q. Have you feen them very often?
A. Several times, fome of them very often.
Q. But you do not recollect whether you ever faw Dunn there?
A. No.
Q. You know Mr. Kinnafton?
A. Yes.
Q. I believe you won't refufe him the teftimony that every man will give in his favour, that he is a man of credit and character?
A. I do not know him, but perfonally.
Q. However you take upon you to fwear there were never any men drilled while you was by?
A. Never.
Q. How many hours were you there at a time?
A. About two hours.
Q. You fay twenty men might be there—cannot you extend their number to fifty or fixty?
A. I may perhaps have feen fifty or fixty.
Q. What is the different object of the focieties? the conftitutional fociety is for a reform in parliament; what was the Reformation Society for?
A. I was not a member of the Reformation Society.

Q. It is commonly called the Subversion or Overthrow Society, is it not?
A. I do not know what you may call it.
Q. Being at these meetings so held jointly, the Reformation and Constitutional Societies, you never knew the objects for which the Reformation Society was formed?
A. I did not attend to the objects of the Reformation Society at all.
Q. Then you do not know the object for which it was formed?
A. How should I when I was not a member of it? they met there to join the Constitutional Society when any member of that society took the chair. I had nothing to do with it, and did not attend to it.
Q. And you were even a stranger to the objects of it?
A. Yes.
Q. You are a partner with Mr. Walker's brother-in-law, and being present at their assemblies, you did not know what they assembled for?
A. I assembled there to meet the Constitutional Society, and their objects were the same I should suppose.

Mr. *George Wakefield*.

Re-examined by Mr. Serjeant *Cockell*.

Q. Although you was not a member of the Reformation Society, but of the Constitutional Society, did you ever when the Reformation Society was there, hear or see any person exercising themselves in arms?
A. Never.

George Clark (sworn.)

Examined by Mr. *Chambre*.

Q. You are a member of the society called the Reformation Society at Manchester?
A. Yes.
Q. When did you become a member of that society?
A. About Easter 1792.
Q. When was the society instituted?
A. Either in Easter week, or about a week before, and I was a member about the second or third meeting.
Q. How often did you meet?
A. I was a very constant attendant.
Q. At what periods did you meet?
A. We had weekly meetings.
Q. Did you continue a pretty constant attending member during the whole time of the existence of that society?

A. I did.

Q. Where did you meet when you firſt became a member?
A. At the Old Boar's head.

Q. Did you remove from that place?
A. Yes, to Stacey's.

Q. What was the occaſion of your removing to John Stacey's?
A. In conſequence of an advertiſement publiſhed by the publicans, we removed to John Stacey's.

Q. Do you know about what time it was you went to John Stacey's?
A. I cannot tell.

Q. Did you continue at John Stacey's?
A. Not long.

Q. Where did you go next?
A. To the houſe of William Gorſe in Newton-ſtreet.

Q. Is that a private or a public houſe?
A. A private houſe.

Q. You know Mr. Walker, Mr. Collier, and Mr. Paul?
A. I do.

Q. Do you know whether they at any time received any invitation to attend the meeting of your ſociety?
A. I cannot ſay I do.

Q. When did you firſt ſee them preſent at your ſociety?
A. I never ſaw them before the 10th of December at Gorſe's.

Q. What did you underſtand them to be?
A. Members of the Conſtitutional Society; I believe Mr. Cheetham was there but I am not confident, the other three were there at that time.

Q. Do you know what was the ſubject of the deliberation of that particular meeting?
A. The particular ſubject of that meeting was, there was a public meeting called at the Bull's-head the day following, to addreſs his Majeſty upon his ſecond proclamation; a motion was made whether we ſhould attend that meeting at the Bull's-head or not; it was unanimouſly negatived.

Q. Did Mr. Walker take any part or aſſign any reaſon?
A. Mr. Walker and Mr. Paul ſpoke againſt attending that meeting, and aſſigned their reaſons.

Mr. *Law.* Does any of our evidence let in this?—we have given no evidence, but of meetings in Mr. Walker's houſe; they are giving evidence of meetings at another place, probably for other purpoſes.

Mr. *Erſkine.* I ſhould have thought this too plain for argument. If my friend inſiſts upon his objection, we muſt be heard upon it; the offence imputed to Mr. Walker is, that a few days after the 11th of December, the witneſs, Dunn, found him harranguing the Reformation Society in the ſeditious manner ſtated by the witneſs, ſpeaking of the King in the manner he has depoſed to, and men exerciſing with arms in his preſence. Is it not evidence, to ſhew that this very Reformation Society was inſtituted for other purpoſes than thoſe imputed to it, and that there was no man who had been ſo counſelled or received any ſuch inſtructions?

Mr. Juſtice *Heath*. I think it is not evidence what they did three days before, becauſe a man may expreſs his loyalty in one meeting, and if he has bad intentions he may go and act traitorouſly in another; I do not ſay that theſe defendants did, I only ſay this to ſhew that it is not evidence.

Mr. *Erſkine*. Though we cannot prove what Mr. Walker ſaid at this meeting, for the reaſon your Lordſhip has been pleaſed to aſſign, yet may we not be permitted to prove that this Reformation Society, within the knowledge of the witneſſes, three days before that time, had no ſuch objects?

Mr. Juſtice *Heath*. I do not care what object they had in meeting, people may meet very innocently, and proceed to criminal acts afterwards.

Mr. *Chambre*. Was that meeting of the 10th of December the laſt meeting you had in the houſe of Gorſe?

A. Yes.

Q. What were the general purpoſes of the inſtitution of that ſociety?

Mr. *Law*. A queſtion couched in words ſo general, I conceive cannot be put to a witneſs, they may examine as to facts, as to what was done and ſaid, what meaſures were adopted by the people there—the purpoſes and objects are matters of the heart.

Mr. Juſtice *Heath*. I think they may ſhew what is the declared purpoſe when people meet together.

Mr. *Erſkine*. We are going to every meeting where Dunn was, to ſhew that no ſuch purpoſes as he ſtates either were the avowed or the expreſſed objects.

Mr. Juſtice *Heath*. Take it up when Dunn came.

Mr. *Erſkine*. If he had ſtated the particular day on which he was at any meeting, we ſhould not have troubled your Lordſhip with any other evidence.

Mr. Juſtice *Heath*. You fixed it by the day after the attack upon Mr. Walker's houſe.

Mr. *Chambre*. The 10th of December you ſay was the laſt meeting you had at Gorſe's houſe; where did you remove to when you left Gorſe's houſe?

A. To Mr. Walker's warehouſe.

Q. How did that happen, and what was the occaſion of that removal?

A. Some perſon expreſſed a wiſh in the Reformation Society ———

Mr. *Law*. That I object to—you removed the ſociety?

Mr. *Chambre*. Was Mr. Walker applied to?

A. Some perſon ſaid ———

Mr. *Law*. Go to the firſt meeting at Mr. Walker's.

Q. When did you firſt meet at Mr. Walker's?

A. On the 11th of December.

Q. And from that time, as long as the ſociety exiſted, you continued to attend the meetings?

A. I continued attending the meetings till the 25th of March, with very great ſtrictneſs.

Mr. *Erſkine*. That comprehends the whole time that Dunn ſpeaks to.

Q. After the 25th of March did you attend?
A. I attended a few times after that, but cannot tell how many.
Q. But with great regularity till the 25th of March?
A. Yes.
Q. How long did you use to attend at a time, as near as you can recollect?
A. It was the general rule to meet at seven, and the business of the meeting to begin at half past; I was scarcely ever out of the meetings at the time the business began.
Q. And did you stay till the conclusion, or near the conclusion?
A. I never, to my knowledge, went away before the conclusion of the meeting.
Q. What were the avowed purposes of this meeting?
A. To obtain a reform in parliament.
Q. Now during all this period of your attendance there, did you ever hear Mr. Walker or any of the defendants in this indictment, propose any other than peaceable means of reform?
A. No, I never did.
Q. Did you ever hear them make use of any expressions that had in your judgment any tendency to excite any body to acts of rebellion?
A. No, I did not.
Q. Was any mention made of an expected invasion of the French, and of any attempts to assist them in that invasion?
A. No, there was not.
Q. Did you ever hear any thing like it proposed at any time?
A. No, I never did.
Q. Had that been the subject of your deliberations, or had such expressions been used by Mr. Walker, or any of the persons there, do you think you must not have heard them, and must not have remembered them?
A. I am certain any thing of that sort could not have happened without my observation, I attended so strictly.
Q. Upon the 11th of December the riot happened, I believe?
A. It did.
Q. Was you in Mr. Walker's house at that time?
A. I was.
Q. What happened on the night of the 11th?
A. About half past six o'clock I went from my house into the town; when I got into the market-place, I saw several people throwing stones at the windows and doors of Messrs. Falkner and Birch's * shop in the market-place; I went as soon as I saw what was going on there, to Mr. Walker's, and I was there till the rioters approached his house; when they first approached it, I was upstairs in the warehouse; I very well recollect there came somebody up and told Mr. Walker the rioters were before his house, and I well recollect he went down, but he was not long before he came up again, and said, they had only broke a few panes of the windows and were gone off again.

* Messrs. Falkner and Birch were stationers in Manchester, and the sole proprietors and publishers of the Manchester Herald.

Q. Did any mifchief happen that night, the 11th?

A. They attacked the houfe four different times; I was up in the warehoufe while it was attacked three times, before I went down; but the fourth time I was in the houfe when it was attacked; it was attacked with very great violence.

Q. On that night were there any arms in the houfe that were ufed for refifting this mob?

A. I faw no arms in the houfe, n'ly a couple of blunderbuffes, and I think I recollect fomething of a piftol, that was all I faw.

Q. Do you know whether any attempt was made on that night to obtain affiftance from the civil power, from the magiftrates; were you prefent at any requifition of that fort?

A. I was not.

Q. After the riot, to the 25th of March, did you attend the meetings at Mr. Walker's?

A. Yes.

Q. Did you fee at any times any arms ufed at Mr. Walker's houfe for any other purpofe than to protect the houfe?

A. No, I never did.

Q. When did you fee any arms there ufed for that purpofe?

A. I never faw any arms but upon the 11th of December.

Q. Was there at any time, to your knowledge, any men exercifed or inftructed in the ufe of arms?

A. No, there never were.

Q. Could fuch a thing poffibly have exifted at any of the meetings, without your knowledge?

A. No, it was impoffible it fhould exift without my knowledge.

Q. Do you know what the arms were that Mr. Walker had in his houfe?

A. I never faw any fire arms, except thefe blunderbuffes, and fome fwivels.

Q. I believe you don't know in what way Mr. Walker became poffeffed of thefe fwivels?

A. No.

Q. But whatever the arms were, were they ever brought out or ufed for the purpofe of exercife, or any other purpofe, to your knowledge, except on the 11th of December?

A. They were not.

Q. This you are perfectly certain of, that there never was any training or exercifing of men there?

A. There never was.

Q. Did you ever hear Mr. Walker, or any body elfe belonging to the fociety, declare a purpofe of that fort?

A. No.

Q. Do you remember Dunn being at any of thefe meetings?

A. I have feen Dunn there.

Q. When he was attending there, when you faw him, can you take upon you to fay, that if any declaration of any purpofe of that fort had been made, or if there had been any exercife of arms, you muft have feen it and known it?

A. Yes.

Q. If you had heard amongst the members of this society any propofition or intention to affift the French in an invafion, would you have continued a member of that society?
A. No, I certainly would not.
Q. Were you prefent at the time when a perfon who has been named, a Mr. Yorke, was at the meeting?
A. Yes, I was.
Q. Do you know whether he attended one or more meetings?
A. I never faw him there but once.
Q. Did he take the chair?
A. There was no perfon in the chair that night to my knowledge.
Q. Did Mr. Yorke talk any thing of vifiting the three kingdoms, to fee whether there were perfons that would affift the French in cafe of an invafion?
A. No, he did not.
Q. Did he fpeak any thing of an invafion of the French with fifty thoufand, or any other number of men?
A. He did not.
Q. Did he exprefs any purpofe or wifh in any way whatever to affift them in any of the three kingdoms?
A. He did not.
Q. If he had made any public declaration of that fort, are you certain you muft have heard him?
A. Yes.

George Clark.

Crofs-examined by Mr. *Wood.*

Q. You continued to meet pretty conftantly from December till the 25th of March, did you?
A. Yes.
Q. You met every night, once a week?
A. I miffed two nights.
Q. Had you a chairman at every time of your meeting?
A. We did not vote a chairman every night.
Q. How happened that?
A. Sometimes we had no bufinefs to do.
Q. How came you to meet fo often as once a week?
A. We met to difcourfe on our own bufinefs, to difcourfe on political matters.
Q. You difcourfed on political matters from half paft feven till nine, and then went away?
A. Yes, we generally broke up about that time.
Q. You never read any thing, I fuppofe?
A. I never heard but very few things read.
Q. There were fome few things read, were there?

A. Yes, I have heard a letter or two read, and I heard an excellent piece that came from Sheffield, figned " A Reformer," read *.

Q. You never heard any thing elfe read?
A. Not to my knowledge.
Q. You mean to fwear you never heard any thing elfe read?
A. No, nothing but that and letters.
Q. You had a good many letters?
A. No, very few.
Q. Who produced thofe letters? did you all produce letters?
A. We had no letter, unlefs it came from Sheffield, or fome other fociety.
Q. How many focieties did you correfpond with?
A. That I cannot tell.
Q. Did you ever come to any refolutions in writing at your meetings?
A. We had general rules that were read every night of our meeting.
Q. Did you come to any refolutions at your meetings?
A. Yes.

Mr. *Erfkine.* You fhall have them all read.
Mr. *Law.* How can you make them evidence?
Mr. *Wood.* Who kept your refolutions?
A. The fecretary.
Q. Who was he?
A. John Cheetham was fecretary one part of the time.
Q. Who was fecretary the other part of the time?
A. John Stacey and George M'Callum.
Q. Where is George M'Callum?
A. I cannot tell?
Q. Is not he gone to America?
A. I do not know.

George Clark.

Re-examined by Mr. *Chambre.*

Q. Did you ever at any time fee Mr. Walker, or any other defendant, do any one act that was inconfiftent with the duty of a peaceable citizen?
A. No.

Mr. *Law.* Does your Lordfhip think it is proper to put fuch a queftion?

Mr. *Erfkine.* Mr. Walker is indicted before your Lordfhip and his country, for having confederated and confpired with the other defendants, and others unknown, to overthrow by force the conftitution of this kingdom. The evidence is, that this confederacy and confpiracy exifted and was brought into overt act, at meet-

---

* See the Appendix, No. xii.

ings, at every one of which this worthy man was present. I say I have a right in defence of my clients, and till his Lordship rules the contrary, I will infist upon that right, that this witnefs shall fay, whether at any of thefe times, he ever heard Mr. Walker utter any word, or fpeak inconfiftent with the duty of a good fubject.

Mr. *Law.* Then I object to that.

Mr. *Erfkine.* Good God! where am I? am I in a Britifh court of juftice? how is a man to defend himfelf under fuch a charge? how are my clients to be exculpated?

Mr. *Law.* By legal evidence.

Mr. Juftice *Heath.* I think that queftion is admiffible enough.

Mr. *Chambre.* Did you at any one of thofe meetings fee Mr. Walker, Mr. Jackfon, Mr. Paul, or any of thofe perfons that are now indicted, do any one act inconfiftent with the character of a peaceable fubject?

A. No; I have often heard Mr. Walker———

Mr. Juftice *Heath.* That is irregular.

Mr. *Erfkine.* Your Lordfhip knows the conftitution of the country gives me no opportunity of addreffing myfelf to any other court for any revifion, and therefore I have a better title to be heard; I will prove that Mr. Walker made ufe of expreffions there of a direct contrary tendency.

Mr. Juftice *Heath.* You fhould have examined to that in chief; you are coming to particulars now upon a re-examination.

Mr. *Erfkine.* It arifes upon Mr. Wood's crofs examination. I am glad to hear that we have your Lordfhip's authority to examine in chief to it; we have a great many more witneffes to examine.

Mr. Juftice *Heath.* If you have a mind, afk that general queftion.

Mr. *Law.* It is a complex queftion, embracing the witneffes idea of what may become an honeft man, pointing at no particular fact or expreffion, which any man may anfwer according to his vague ideas of propriety.

Mr. *Erfkine.* When a man is indicted for exciting fedition and rebellion, is it not evidence to fhew that he held a language directly repugnant to any fuch idea? If he had faid God blefs the King, would not that be evidence?

Mr. Juftice *Heath.* If it was at that meeting.

Mr. *Law.* If it goes to the whole tenor of his conduct; but a man fhall not be juftified by faying God blefs the King, in the ftreet, when he has been damning him in his houfe.

Mr. Juftice *Heath.* Afk him to their general declarations.

Mr. *Chambre.* At thofe meetings, when Mr. Walker was prefent, did you hear him fay or do any thing that had a tendency to difturb the peace of the kingdom; I am examining to the meetings of the Reformation Society between the 11th of December and the 25th of March?

A. When Mr. Walker came to our meetings he generally addreffed us to attend to peace and good order.

Q. Did you, or did you not hear Mr. Walker fay any thing inconfiftent with peace and good order, or any thing againft the King and his government, or any thing that tended to fubvert it—

or say any thing to excite people to take up arms against the King, or to destroy the constitution?

A. I never did in my life.

Mr. *Erskine.* Whether the witness has not a right to go on and say, but on the contrary he said so and so, am I not at liberty to ask that?

Mr. Justice *Heath.* Not in this stage.

One of the Jury. What is the height of the warehouse in which you used to meet?

A. I never took notice how high it was, how many pair of stairs up.

Q. The height of the room from the floor to the cieling?

Mr. *Erskine.* We will give evidence of that.

James Lomax (sworn.)

Examined by Mr. *Lloyd.*

Q. Where do you live?
A. In Salford.
Q. Are you a member of any of these societies?
A. Yes, the Reformation Society.
Q. When did you become a member of that society?
A. The first night I met, was the Monday night after Mr. Walker was so ill used at the riots in Manchester—the 17th of December I think, and I entered about three nights after; we met every Monday night.
Q. Did you often attend the societies?
A. Yes, I think I did not miss above once, till the latter end of March, or the beginning of April, for there were some resolutions signed, that were put into the last paper Mr. Falkner printed; I believe I did not miss but one night; that was somewhere towards February, but I am not certain which night it was.
Q. At what time did you generally go to the meeting?
A. About seven o'clock; the last Monday in the month was my box night, I either then went at eight, or at seven and left the place at eight.
Q. How long did you stay?
A. I generally staid till the end, till they were all going, and I saw nothing else likely to be done.
Q. What was the avowed object of this society?
A. To gain a reform in parliament.
Q. Do you know Dunn by sight?
A. Yes.
Q. Did you ever see him there?
A. Yes, and one night he and I were a good deal together; I recollected him when I saw him to-day: I have never seen him since.
Q. You have seen Mr. Walker there?
A. Yes.

Q. Have you ever heard Mr. Walker damn the King?
A. No.
Q. Did you ever see any persons exercise with arms there?
A. No.
Q. Did you ever see any firelocks there?
A. No; only the first night I went, I stopped by the desire of Mr. Walker that night, for he expected another riot; they broke one of his windows, we went out, and whether Mr. Walker had a pistol in his hand when we went out to find the person, or not, I cannot tell; I saw nothing except in his warehouse, there were six pieces of some sort, but not firelocks.
Q. What do you call them? what length are they?
A. About this length *(describing them to be about eighteen inches long.)*
Q. You never saw any person exercising there with firelocks?
A. Never.
Q. Did you ever hear any recommendation of beginning to exercise?
A. No.
Q. If there had been such in the society, you must have seen it?
A. Yes, and I would have scorned to have tarried in it.
Q. Did you ever hear Mr. Walker, or any other, say they would overthrow the constitution?
A. I never did.
Q. Would you have stayed in the society if such a proposal had been made?
A. I do not believe I should one moment.
Q. Did you ever hear Mr. Walker or the others who were there, say or do any thing inconsistent with the duty of good subjects?
A. No; I have heard Mr. Walker many times advise us to be peaceable, and say many times he had no doubt we should be peaceable: I never saw any thing in that society that they need to be ashamed of either before God or man.
Q. Did you ever hear them talk of exciting the people to sedition or rebellion?
A. No.
Q. Or exciting the people to take up arms?
A. No.
Q. Did you ever hear them talk of assisting the French?
A. I never did.
Q. If you had heard them talk of assisting the French would you have stayed with them?
A. No; my principles are those that I would neither have war offensive nor defensive.
Q. Do you know Mr. Collier?
A. I believe I do; he is a tall man.
Q. Do you know what religion he is of?
A. A Quaker.
Q. Have you heard him swear often?
A. No, I never did in my life.

Cross-examined by Mr. *Topping*.

Q. Where do you live?
A. In Salford.
Q. What business are you?
A. A weaver.
Q. You had attended these meetings then before you became a member?
A. Yes, I think it was the third night, but I cannot be positive.
Q. Then people were admitted to attend these meetings who were not actually members?
A. I never saw any denied; I have taken a man twice myself.
Q. They were admitted to these meetings, although they were not members?
A. Yes.
Q. Before you became a member you was admitted, and after you became a member you took people with you?
A. I took one man with me that had a desire to go.
Q. Upon the 17th of December you became a member?
A. No.
Q. You said you went on the 17th, and went before you became a member?
A. No, I never attended till the 17th of December.
Q. When did you become a member?
A. I believe it was the third night after.
Q. Did Mr. Walker ask you to become a member?
A. No, I went of my own free will; I don't know that any man asked me.
Q. Do you remember Paine's works being read there?
A. No, I never saw them there.
Q. Did you hear them read?
A. I never did hear them read there.
Q. Did you ever hear any part of Paine's book read there?
A. No.
Q. Have not you, upon your oath, heard books read there, which you understood to be Paine's books?
A. I never did.
Q. That you swear?
A. I do; I have heard books read I did not know whose they were; if they had been Paine's, they would have mentioned that, I suppose?
Q. You mean to say no books of Paine's were read there?
A. If it had been Paine's Rights of Man, I should have known that.
Q. Was it your knowledge of the contents of that book that entitled you to be a member of this society?
A. No.

Q. Had you the knowledge of Paine's book before you became a member of this society, or after?
A. Before, I believe.
Q. Upon your oath, have you never heard Jackson, one of the defendants, read Paine's Rights of Man there?
A. No, I never have that I know of.
Q. You say you know Paine's Rights of Man perfectly well?
A. Yes.
Q. Will you venture to swear that you never heard Jackson read any part of that book there?
A. I never have as I know of.
Q. Don't you know?
A. He has read books.
Q. Has he read books repeatedly at these meetings?
A. I only heard one or two read, and those were abstracts.
Q. Were they not abstracts out of Paine's Rights of Man?
A. They were not.
Q. What was the subject he was reading about to you?
A. There was one book, I remember, that came from London, concerning the unequal representation of the people, that came from the Friends of the People.

Mr. *Topping*. That came from the Friends of the People!

Mr. *Erskine*. I presume it did, as I believe a packet was transmitted from the Friends of the People to the Constitutional Society in Manchester. I am a member of the Friends of the People, and if you have any question to ask relative to that society, swear me, and I will answer them.

Mr. *Topping*. Who read that?
A. Mr. Jackson.
Q. Was he the general reader at the meeting? who read besides him?
A. I have heard Mr. Walker read newspapers.
Q. Sometimes Mr. Walker read, and sometimes Mr. Jackson?
A. We had nothing else to pass our time away with; and to see how public affairs were going on.

James Lomax.

Re-examined by Mr. *Lloyd*.

Q. What night was it you saw Mr. Walker go out, and you suppose with a pistol?
A. It was on the 17th of December.
Q. Were the riots then continued?
A. They broke one of Mr. Walker's windows that night.
Q. You were not a member then?
A. No.
Q. You went as a friend to defend Mr. Walker's house?
A. I did.
Q. The book you heard read was, you say, the publication by the Society of the Friends of the People in London?
A. It was.

James Roberts, (sworn.)

Examined by Mr. *Vaughan*.

Q. Are you a member of the Reformation Society at Manchester?
A. Yes.
Q. How long have you been a member of that society?
A. I entered, I believe, on the 21st of December 1792.
Q. Have you regularly attended the meetings of that society?
A. I attended very regularly.
Q. From this time in December till what time?
A. Till the 10th day of June 1793.
Q. What was the avowed object of the meetings of this society?
A. To obtain, by constitutional means, a fair and adequate representation of the people.
Q. Do you know Mr. Thomas Walker?
A. Yes.
Q. Have you seen him at your Reformation Society?
A. Very frequently.
Q. Up to what time did you see Mr. Walker there?
A. Till the 29th day of April.
Q. Have you seen Thomas Dunn there?
A. Yes, I have.
Q. Have you been present when Dunn was present?
A. Yes.
Q. Did you at any of these times, when Thomas Dunn was present, see any exercising of men with arms?
A. No, never.
Q. Or at any other time, when Dunn was not there, did you see any exercising of men with arms?
A. Never.
Q. Did you at any time hear any language whatever from Mr. Thomas Walker, or any other persons, inciting the society to exercise with arms, for any purpose, and what?
A. No, I never saw them exercise with arms.
Q. In what place did this Reformation Society meet?
A. In Mr. Thomas Walker's warehouse.
Q. Up stairs, or below stairs?
A. Above stairs.
Q. Do you know the height of this warehouse, from the floor to the ceiling?
A. I do not.
Q. Did you ever hear from Mr. Thomas Walker, or any other persons whatever, any language relative to cutting off the head of the King, or any thing of a similar tendency?
A. Never in my life.

K

Q. Did you ever hear or see from Mr. Thomas Walker, any language or conduct whatever, that tended to incite the people against the government, or to any similar purpose?

A. I never did.

Q. Did you ever see in Mr. Thomas Walker, or any other persons whatever attending that society, any conduct unbecoming honest men and good subjects?

A. Never.

Q. Did you ever see any arms at any time in the warehouse?

A. Just after the riot I saw some pieces of cannon; there were five or six.

Q. What sort of cannon were they, twenty-four or forty eight pounders?

A. I do not properly understand them.

Q. What length were they?

A. About three quarters of a yard long.

Q. Did you ever see any musketry there?

A. No, never but on the twelfth of December.

Q. You never saw any musketry at any time during your attendance, but on the night of the riot, or the night after?

A. No, that was one musket in Mr. Walker's kitchen.

Q. How often did you see that?

A. Never but once.

James Roberts.

Cross-examined by Mr. *Johnson.*

Q. What are you?
A. I am in a warehouse.
Q. What trade are you?
A. I am in a warehouse.
Q. What are you?
A. A warehouseman.
Q. Who do you live with?
A. Messrs. Nichols and Roberts.
Q. Who introduced you into this Society?
A. I was not introduced by any person.
Q. How came you to go there?
A. I went there the 12th of December, the night following the first riot.
Q. Were there more riots than one?
A. The mob met two days together.
Q. I asked who introduced you to this society; you said, nobody. When did you go to it first?
A. The 12th of December was the first time I went to Mr. Walker's.
Q. When was the first time you went to the society?
A. The 20th of December.
Q. Was you a member then?

A. No, I did not become a member until the 31ſt of December.

Q. You ſaid, juſt now, you became a member on the 31ſt January 1793.

Mr. Serjeant *Cockell.* You have taken him down wrong.

Mr. *Johnſon.* What was your inducement to become a member of this Reformation Society?

A. They wiſhed a fair repreſentation of the people in parliament.

Mr. Juſtice *Heath.* Don't let us enquire into that.

Mr. *Erſkine.* It is evidence for the defendants, and if the gentlemen chooſe to aſk it, I have a right to the evidence.

A. On the 12th of December, as I was at work, I ſaw a great concourſe of people met in the market-place; I thought there would be a riot in the evening; I went out, went into the church yard, and went to Mr. Walker's houſe that night; and I ſaw ſuch conduct in Mr. Walker, and the people that were there, that it made me determine to enter among them.

Mr. *Johnſon.* You ſay you ſaw no exerciſing, but you did ſee arms?

A. I never ſaw any fire-arms, but one muſket?

Q. Did you ſee no other fire-arms?

A. Yes, ſix pieces of cannon.

Q. Were they large enough to carry a pound ball?

A. I cannot tell, I was never uſed to them.

Q. Did you ſee any blunderbuſſes there?

A. I do not recollect ſeeing any blunderbuſſes there.

Q. Did you ever hear any books read there?

A. I heard one book read.

Q. What was it?

A. They called it the Iriſh Addreſs to the Scotch.

Q. Who read that?

A. Mr. Walker did.

Q. Perhaps you cannot recollect any particular paſſage in it?

A. No.

Mr. *Erſkine.* I dare ſay you recollect that is not evidence, therefore you aſk it.

Mr. *Law.* It confirms him as to the reading of books there.

Mr. Juſtice *Heath.* There is no doubt, your witneſs was there.

Mr. *Johnſon.* You heard that read by Mr. Walker?

A. Yes.

Mr. *Vaughan.* They did not ſhoulder theſe ſwivels, did they?

A. No, never.

Mary Denham (ſworn).

Examined by Mr. *Erſkine.*

Q. How long have you lived as a ſervant with Mr. Walker?

A. For two years upon the 10th of March laſt.

Q. Do you remember the attack made upon your maſter's houſe?

A. Yes.

Q. Was you in the house at that time?
A. Yes.
Q. I suppose you was pretty much frightened?
A. Yes, I was.
Q. Do you remember any cannon?
A. Yes.
Q. When were these cannon brought to town?
A. The day after the riot.
Q. Where were they before?
A. In the country.
Q. At Barlow-Hall, where Mr. Walker lives?
A. Yes.
Q. They are little things upon carriages?
A. Yes.
Q. They were brought into town the day after the riot?
A. Yes.
Q. Before the time that these cannon came, do you remember seeing fire-arms in your master's house?
A. No.
Q. Was you admitted to all the parts of the warehouse, and the house—you went where you pleased, I suppose?
A. Yes.
Q. Did you ever see any men exercising with arms there?
A. No.
Q. Did you ever hear of any thing like it?
A. No.
Q. Did you ever see any arms there before the time of the riots?
A. No.
Q. If any such exercise of people with arms had taken place, must you not have known it?
A. Yes.
Q. Why should you have known it?
A. They could not do it in the warehouse, or house, without my seeing or hearing it.
Q. Did you ever either see any such thing done, or hear of its being done?
A. No, never.
Q. Can you take upon you to swear that it was not done?
A. Yes.
Q. After the riots, we understand these cannon, and some muskets, and other arms were brought for the purpose of defending the house?
A. Yes.
Q. What was done with them after the 12th of December?
A. They went into the country again I believe.
Q. What was it that went into the country again?
A. The cannon.
Q. What became of the blunderbusses, pistols, and muskets?
A. I never saw any.
Q. You never saw any after the riot, nor before?
A. No.
Q. You don't know where these cannon went to?
A. No, I saw no more of them.

Mary Denham.

Cross examined by Mr. *James.*

Q. Were you a member of any of these Reformation Societies?
A. No.
Q. Did you ever attend them?
A. No.
Q. How could you tell what was going forward at any of those meetings? you did not generally attend the warehouse.
A. No.
Q. Your business was in the house?
A. Yes.
Q. But how can you pretend to say what was done in the warehouse; they might have been in the warehouse for what you know?
A. Not to exercise they could not; I must have seen them through the windows.
Q. Have you been accustomed to see men exercise?
A. I have seen the soldiers exercise.
Q. They did not always fire when they exercised?
A. No.
Q. Have you not seen them exercise, when they made very little noise?
A. No, I do not know that I have.
Q. Have you never seen them present, and rise, and kneel, and so on; you say there were no blunderbusses or muskets?
A. I never saw any.
Q. And if there was, you must have seen them, must you?
A. Yes.
Mr. *Erskine.* Is there not a double light through the warehouse?
A. Yes.
Q. If they had been exercising with fire-arms there, must you not have seen and heard them?
A. Yes.

Martha Wilkinson (sworn).

Examined by Mr. Sergeant *Cockell.*

Q. I understand you live in the service of Mr. Walker; you attend the Miss Walkers, as their maid?
A. Yes.
Q. How long have you lived in Mr. Walker's service?
A. More than three years and a half.
Q. Where was you at the time of the riot, the first night Mr. Walker's house was attacked?

A. At Barlow.
Q. Mr. Walkers country refidence?
A. Yes.
Q. When did you return from Barlow?
A. The day after.
Q. How long did you continue after you had returned from Barlow?
A. Till the beginning of May.
Q. During that period you lived in his houfe at Manchefter?
A. I did.
Q. Do you remember after your return from Barlow, whether any arms of any fort were fent for?
A. No.
Q. Do you remember the cannon?
A. Yes.
Q. Where did they come from?
A. From Barlow, before I came.
Q. How long before?
A. The fame day I came.
Q. That was the day after the riot?
A. Yes.
Q. You know Mr. Walker's warehoufe?
A. Yes.
Q. Can you from any room in the houfe fee into the warehoufe?
A. Yes.
Q. Is the warehoufe fo near to that part of the houfe, from whence you can fee into the warehoufe, that if any noife, for inftance the clattering of ramrods, or any thing of that fort had happened, you could have heard them?
A. Yes.
Q. You have feen foldiers exercife at Manchefter?
A. I cannot fay I ever did.
Q. But if there had been any noife of that fort, you was near enough to have heard, and to have feen?
A. Yes.
Q. Did you ever hear or fee at any time in your life, any men exercifing in arms at Mr. Walker's?
A. No, never.
Q. If fuch a thing had happened when thefe weekly meetings were held, muft you not at fome time or other have heard it?
A. Moft certainly I muft.
Q. And you are prepared, fafely and confcientioufly to fwear, that no fuch thing happened?
A. I am.
Q. Defcribe the fituation of this window?
A. There is but a narrow yard that parts the warehoufe and the houfe, and the windows of the warehoufe, and the windows of the room in which I was, were oppofite.
Q. Then if any thing of that fort had happened, you muft have feen and heard it?
A. I certainly fhould.
Q. Do you know the height of the warehoufe?
A. I do not.

Q. You know the gentlemen who came to Mr. Walker's; you know that clubs were held there?
A. Yes.
Q. I confine myself to the time during the holding of the clubs; did you ever hear any noise then of arms?
A. Never.
Q. Did you ever see any exercising of men at those times, or at any other?
A. Never.

Martha Wilkinson.

Cross-examined by Mr. *Law.*

Q. In what room do you usually live?
A. In the nursery; the nursery in general.
Q. Is the nursery higher or lower than the warehouse?
A. From the nursery windows we can see into several rooms of the warehouse.
Q. Is it higher or lower?
A. It is higher than one part of the warehouse, and lower than another.
Q. Is it as high as the upper room of the warehouse?
A. It is not quite so high.
Q. Will you say, that you can conveniently, from that room, see into the upper room of the warehouse?
A. We can see into it.
Q. Can you see from one end to the other of the warehouse, from the nursery?
A. Yes, from one end to the other of the upper warehouse?
Q. The upper warehouse of all?
A. Yes.
Q. And was you every night, for forty nights together, when these persons were there, so watching their proceedings, that you could know if a person had put a musket to his shoulder?
A. I was not constantly watching, but I have no doubt if there had been such a thing I should have known it.
Q. Did you observe all that passed there?
A. We frequently watched them.
Q. What did they do when you watched them?
A. We never saw but they were sitting still.
Q. Talking?
A. Yes.
Q. You saw books, I take for granted?
A. No, I did not.
Q. You never saw any thing read?
A. Never.
Q. But if there had been Paine's book, or any other book read, you must have seen it?
A. I did not see any book.
Q. If they had been so employed, you must have seen that too?

A. I cannot ſay.
Q. Why could you not ſee a book held up, juſt as well as ſee a muſket held up?
A. I never did ſee a book read.
Q. How many might there be in the room at a time?
A. I cannot ſay the exact number.
Q. You have ſeen Dunn there?
A. No.
Q. Were there twenty, thirty, forty, fifty there?
A. I cannot tell.
Q. Do you think there were ſo many as forty or fifty?
A. I do not know.
Q. Had you never the curioſity to count them when there was a good number?
A. Never.
Q. But if there had been books, you think you muſt have ſeen them, and you never ſaw any read?
A. I never ſaw any book read.

Martha Wilkinſon.

Re-examined by Mr. Serjeant *Cockell.*

Q. From this nurſery, in which you frequently were, in the evenings, if there had been men exerciſing, you muſt have ſeen them?
A. Yes.
Q. What ſort of windows are the warehouſe windows?
A. Nearly the length of the warehouſe.

Francis Roberts (ſworn.)

Examined by Mr. *Chambre.*

Q. You are a ſervant to Mr. Walker?
A. Yes.
Q. How long have you lived with him?
A. I came to live with Mr. Walker in the year 1791; I have lived with him ever ſince.
Q. You were ſervant to him, of courſe, when the riots happened in Mancheſter?
A. I was.
Q. Mr. Walker has a houſe at Mancheſter, and a country-houſe at Barlow?
A. He has.

Q. At the time of the riots were you at Manchester, or Barlow?
A. At Barlow.
Q. When did you come from Barlow?
A. The morning following.
Q. Do you know what fire arms Mr. Walker had for the protection of both his houses?
A. There was nothing for the protection of his house except two pistols, and two blunderbusses, and two fowling pieces that I ever saw.
Q. Had he any swivels?
A. Yes, half a dozen.
Q. Where were the swivels at the time when the riot happened?
A. At Barlow-hall.
Q. When were they removed from Barlow to Manchester?
A. The day after the riots.
Q. You don't know how he became possessed of those swivels?
A. I do not.
Q. When you came from Barlow, how long did you continue at Manchester?
A. We came the 12th of December, and returned back the 5th of May.
Q. Immediately after you came on the 12th of December, and for some time after, was there any watch kept at Mr. Walker's house, to prevent any mischief being done to the house—did people sit up all night?
A. Yes, they did.
Q. Did you sit up for the protection of the house sometimes?
A. Yes.
Q. How long were they obliged, for the security of the house, to keep up this sort of watch?
A. For the course of a month, or thereabouts.
Q. Were you often among those that sat up?
A. I was.
Q. Of course you were in the house at all the meetings of the Reformation Society, that took place between the 12th of December and the 5th of May?
A. I was.
Q. Had you ever occasion to go into the room where these meetings were held?
A. I had frequent occasion.
Q. Were these meetings held with open doors, or were the doors locked?
A. I always found the doors wide open.
Q. There was no sort of secrecy about the purposes of their meeting?
A. Not to my knowledge.
Q. Have you stayed any time when people were in the room, so as to hear the conversation that passed?
A. I cannot say that I have.
Q. Did you ever at any time hear any expressions made use of, damning the King?

A. Nothing of the fort.
Q. Did you ever hear any expreffions of any fort made ufe of, to incite any of the people there to break the peace?
A. I have no knowledge of any thing of the fort.
Q. Was there any exercife of men with guns or other arms?
A. Nothing of the fort.
Q. Do you think you muft have known it, if any fuch thing had been practifed in the place where thefe people met, or in any part of your mafter's houfe?
A. I am fure fuch things could not be made ufe of, but I fhould have come to the knowledge of it, fome how or other.
Q. Did you at any time whatever, fee or hear any thing done or faid there, that had any tendency to difturb the public peace?
A. I never did.

Francis Roberts.

Crofs-examined by Mr. *Wood.*

Q. How many people might there be at thofe meetings when you faw them?
A. There might be twenty or thirty, and fometimes more.
Q. How many men do you think there might be, fifty or fixty, perhaps?
A. I believe not fo many.
Q. How many do you think?
A. There might be thirty five, or fo.
Q. Is that the moft you ever faw?
A. I do not know in particular that it is.
Q. Have you not feen fixty, or more, there?
A. No.
Q. You won't go higher than thirty-five?
A. No, I will not.
Q. Did you know thofe people that had got there?
A. No.
Q. I believe you was very feldom at thofe meetings; did you ever ftay a meeting through, from beginning to end?
A. No.
Q. How long might you ftay at a time?
A. Three or four minutes, or fo, while I delivered my meffage.
Q. When you ftayed up to protect this houfe, what had you to protect it with?
A. We had a fword or two.
Q. How many might ftay with you? did any of the people that attended thefe meetings ftay with you?
A. They did.
Q. The Reformation Society ftayed with you, did they?
A. Some of thofe people that met in the warehoufe.

Q. How many nights might they stay up with you?
A. I cannot pretend to say how many.
Q. How many may you have had at a time to stay up with you?
A. Four or five.
Q. Not always the same people, I suppose?
A. No.

Francis Roberts.

Re-examined by Mr. *Chambre.*

Q. You never particularly, I suppose, counted the number, to know exactly how many there might be?
A. I never did.

Mr. *Edward Green* (sworn.)

Examined by Mr. *Lloyd.*

Q. You, I believe, were apprentice to Mr. Walker, and brought up in his warehouse?
A. Yes.
Q. How long have you been with him?
A. It will be eight years in July.
Q. Do you remember the night of the riots?
A. Yes.
Q. Do you remember whether there were any arms got to defend Mr. Walker's house?
A. Yes, there were some got.
Q. Do you know what arms they were?
A. They were muskets.
Q. Were there any swivels?
A. No.
Q. Not that night?
A. No.
Mr. Justice *Heath.* How many muskets?
A. I do not know the number.
Mr. *Lloyd.* Were you in the house the first night of the riot?
A. I was.
Q. Do you know when the swivels were bought?
A. They were a present to Master Walker, by Mr. Jackson; they were bought at Mr. Livesey's sale.
Q. Do you know any occasion upon which those swivels were fired?
A. I remember they were fired upon the anniversary of the repeal of the fustian tax.
Q. At any other time?
A. I was not present at any other time.

Q. What is your bufinefs at Mr. Walker's, chiefly?
A. In the foreign counting houfe.
Q. Is that up ftairs, or below, in his warehoufe?
A. Up ftairs.

Mr. Juftice *Heath.* Do you live in the houfe?
A. I lived in the houfe five years.

Mr. *Lloyd.* In what part of the warehoufe is the foreign counting-houfe?
A. It looks towards Salford, up two pair of ftairs.
Q. Do you know the room where the focieties met?
A. It was in a room up another pair of ftairs, where the focieties met.
Q. Have you ever had occafion to go into that room when they were met.
A. I had frequent occafions to go up to Mr. Walker upon bufinefs?
Q. Did you find the door either locked or faftened?
A. Never.
Q. Did they feem to be about fecret bufinefs?
A. Not at all.
Q. Did you go in without interruption?
A. Yes.
Q. Have you had occafion to go in more than once in an evening?
A. I may have gone two or three times, not finding Mr. Walker in the firft time.
Q. How near is that room to the room where you ufed to fit writing?
A. Up another pair of ftairs.
Q. Is part of that room, over the room that you was in?
A. It is.
Q. Did you ever fee any men exercifing with arms when you went up?
A. Never.
Q. When you were writing, did your ever hear any arms clafhing?
A. Never.
Q. Were there carpets upon the floor, or any thing of that kind, to prevent the found?
A. No.
Q. I underftand that you never faw any men exercifing with arms?
A. Never.
Q. Do you know what is the height of that room?
A. I do not know.
Q. Do you know whether it is fuch a room that a man could fhoulder a firelock?
A. I do not know; I never took particular notice.
Q. Did you fend word before you went in, or go in without giving notice?
A. Without giving notice.
Q. When you went in, did you hear any converfation—did you ever hear Mr. Walker damn the King?
A. No,

Q. Or talk of overturning the conſtitution?
A. Never.
Q. Did you hear any converſation of aiding and aſſiſting the French?
A. No.
Q. You never heard any thing of the kind?
A. No.
Q. When you went in, did they ſeem inſtantly to ceaſe their converſation, or to go on with it?
A. They went on with the buſineſs they were about.
Q. Whenever you went in, did you hear Mr. Walker, or any other perſon, ſay any thing to excite diſturbance of the peace?
A. Not at all.
Q. Or exciting them to take up arms to aid the French?
A. No, never.
Q. Or for any other purpoſe?
A. No, by no means, I never heard any thing of the kind.
Q. Or to overthrow the conſtitution?
A. No.

Mr. *Edward Green.*

Croſs-examined by Mr. *Topping.*

Q. If I underſtand you, you have been ſeveral years with Mr. Walker?
A. Yes, I have known Mr. Walker eleven years.
Q. You was a perſon, therefore, perfectly well known as one of Mr. Walker's family?
A. Yes.
Q. Can you take upon you to ſay, how many people you have ever ſeen aſſembled at any one time?
A. Very likely ſeventeen, eighteen, or twenty.
Q. Will you take upon yourſelf to ſay, you have not ſeen to the number of fifty or ſixty at a time?
A. Upon the night of the riots there were a good many.
Q. Can you take upon you to ſay, you have not ſeen to the number of fifty or ſixty aſſembled?
A. I will take upon me to ſwear I have not ſeen, what I conceive to be, ſuch a number as that.
Q. You don't mean to ſay you can form any accurate eſtimate of the number?
A. No.
Q. You was not a member of this ſociety?
A. I was not.
Q. You never went up to this room, unleſs you had occaſion to ſpeak to Mr. Walker, then you went, and he was called out to you?
A. I always went in to him.

Q. My friend has asked you as to having heard, or not, expressions used about the King; now can you take upon you to swear what they were doing, from what you heard?

A. Their conversation seemed to turn upon the question of a reform in parliament.

Q. Whether you mean to swear, that you knew or ever heard from any individual there, any particular expressions used at all that you can relate to the Jury?

A. I do not.

Q. You was not a member of the society?

A. No.

Q. Your object in going there was not to learn what they were doing?

A. No.

Q. When you did go there, it was merely to speak to Mr. Walker about his own business as a merchant?

A. Yes.

Q. What size is the room in which this society was held?

A. It is a long room.

Q. And will hold a great number of people, will it not?

A. It will hold a good many people.

Q. Is it the length, or half the length of this room?

A. I think it is nearly the length of this room.

Q. Is there not another room upon the same floor; does all the attic story make only one room?

A. There is another room.

Q. There is another room upon the same floor, besides the room in which the society was held?

A. Yes, there is.

Q. You said you thought part of it was over the counting-house where you are?

A. Yes, part of it is over that room.

Mr. *Edward Green.*

Re-examined by Mr. *Lloyd.*

Q. The reason why you think the warehouse is over the counting house is, that both rooms look into Salford?

A. Yes both rooms come to the end of the building.

Q. Was it any part of your business to see that all the fires were out in this warehouse, and to lock up at night?

A. It is my general custom to go through the warehouse, and to lock it up.

Q. Did you find any arms lying there, when you went through the rooms to lock all up?

A. Never.

Q. Did you go into this room generally?

A. Yes, I did.

Q. And you did not see any arms lying there?

A. Never.

Mr. *George Duckworth* (sworn.)

Examined by Mr. *Vaughan*.

Q. Are you acquainted with the houfe of Mr. Walker, at Man-chefter?
A. I am.
Q. You are alfo acquainted with the warehoufe of that houfe, and the height of it?
A. Yes, Mr. Walker took me through the houfe and warehoufe a few days ago, to fhew them to me; I had not feen the warehoufe before, only occafionally when I went on bufinefs. Mr. Walker fhewed me the different rooms of the warehoufe upon every ftory. I meafured the height of two ftories, which appeared to be the higheft, and the loweft. The higheft room, to the beft of my re-collection (for I did not expect to be examined here) was nine feet high between the beams, and eight feet fix inches high under the beams.
Mr. *Law.* You did not meafure them?
A. Yes, I did.
Q. Did you make any minute?
A. No. The loweft ftory was feven feet fix inches high under the beams, and eight feet between the beams; I took a mufket out of the room in which Mr. Walker had put the arms, and fixed the bayonet, to fhoulder it: when I fhouldered it, the point of the bayonet touched the ceiling: if I had thrown it up to my fhoulder in the manner they do in the manual exercife, the bayonet would have ftuck into the ceiling; I could not poife it. This was the higheft room in the warehoufe. The rooms in the uppermoft ftory are the higheft.

Mr. *George Duckworth.*

Crofs-examined by Mr. *Law.*

Q. You had no idea of giving any account of this at Lancafter, when you made the meafurement?
A. No. I defired Mr. Walker to get fome perfon to make the meafurement.
Q. Are you not the attorney for Mr. Walker?
A. I am, but I did not examine the whole of the evidence. Mr. Seddon examined fome of the witneffes.
Q. You fay you made no minute in writing of this?
A. I did not.
Q. Where did you get the mufket that you tried with?

A. Out of the room where Mr. Walker had the small collection of arms, which he informed me were what he had at the time of the riots.

Q. So you had a musket !
A. Yes.

Q. How many did you see in the armoury ?
A. About a dozen, I believe, of one sort or other. The arms were covered with dust. The room was full of dust. The arms were of different sorts.

Q. There were twelve muskets?
A. No, not twelve muskets, but different kinds of fire-arms.

Q. With bayonets all ?
A. There were some musketoons with spring bayonets.

Mr. *Walker.* I have an inventory in my pocket, of the arms I had at the time of the riots; I have the arms *now*. The inventory *(offering it to Mr Law)* is very much at your service.

Mr. *Law.* The beam of this room comes very deep down, does it ?
A. About six inches.

Q. Supposing there had been no beams coming down, the room would have been the height of nine feet?
A. Yes.

Q. What did you measure with ?
A. Mr. Walker had a four-foot rule.

Q. You made no minute at the time ?
A. I did not.

Q. Did you advise a carpenter to be sent for to measure it ?
A. I desired Mr. Walker would get some person to measure it.

Mr. *Duckworth*.

Re-examined by Mr. *Vaughan*.

Q. What arms were they that you saw there ? were they different sorts of arms ?
A. A few muskets, a few musketoons, ————

Q. What are musketoons something of the nature of a blunderbuss ?
A. Yes.

Mr. Justice *Heath*. There is one objection, I should be glad to hear what Mr. Law says upon it—it struck me early in the course of this business—*I did not mention it out of tenderness to the defendant, that he might have an opportunity of clearing his character, by calling his witnesses, but it appears to me that this can be nothing else than high treason.*

Mr. *Law.* I submit to your Lordship, that it is not high treason; but at the same time, if these facts could be so understood, the crown might prosecute as for a misdemeanor; that was settled in the cafe of the King againft Hampden *, and it has been laid down in a great number of cafes. I could cite authorities from Lord Chief Juftice Hale, and other books, where the Crown has profecuted as for a mifdemeanor—that the crown, in cafes of felony, might drop fome of the circumftances, and profecute as for a mifdemeanor—the crown may elect to profecute the crime in its mildeft form. This is a point of fuch magnitude, and having been folemnly decided in cafes I could refer to in the STATE TRIALS, I beg your Lordfhip to have the goodnefs to let this be found upon a fpecial verdict.

Mr. *Erfkine*. No—no.

* The precedent here alluded to, is the trial of Mr. Hampden, for a mifdemeanor, in the latter end of the reign of *Charles the fecond*, February the 6th, 1683, before JUDGE JEFFERIES; when Mr. Hampden was fined by him and the reft of the Judges of the King's-Bench, in the fum of FORTY THOUSAND POUNDS!

Mr. Hampden remarked to the court, that his father being alive, his fortune was but fmall, and that merely a life eftate. To this Mr. Juftice Withins faid, that they could not take cognizance of what his eftate was; the punifhment was to be proportioned to the offence, and the Chief Juftice (JEFFERIES) added, that confidering *fome verdicts*, this would be thought *a moderate fine*.

On paffing this fentence, Mr. Hampden was told by the Court, that the matter of the offence was fuch as would have made him guilty of HIGH TREASON, had there been two witneffes. The effence of a crime therefore *(according to this precedent)* does not confift in the nature of the act committed, but is to be *at one time* HIGH TREASON, *at another fomething elfe*, as the profecutor is prepared with one or more witneffes to prove it.

Mr. Hampden remained in prifon, and under execution for the fine, till the 30th of December, 1685, *the firft year of James the fecond*, when a new witnefs appearing, he was *again* indicted for *the fame offence*, but then laid as HIGH TREASON. " His friends offered money for his pardon to fome
" in power, who were the Lord *(Judge)* JEFFERIES, and Mr. Petre, the
" fum was SIX THOUSAND POUNDS, *and that was effectual*. It is not poffible
" for a man to fuffer more than he did."

" By the help of the money, on condition he would plead guilty to his in-
" dictment, he was to come off; whereupon, pleading guilty, he was
" difcharged; paying 300l. or 400l. to *Burton* and *Graham* for the charge
" of his pardon."

" His abject fubmiffion did indeed procure him a pardon; but the fhame
" of fuch a mean behaviour fo funk and difordered his fpirits, that he was
" never quite right after it; and about ten years after he cut his own
" throat." *State Trials*, Vol. III. page 823. Vol. IV. page 210, and Vol. VIII. page 480.

The fine of FORTY THOUSAND POUNDS, without regarding the amount of a man's fortune, and the doctrine of converting high treafon into a mifdemeanor, both ftand upon the fame precedent—The one is *as juftifiable* as the other.

But is it confiftent with the fpirit of the laws of England, that the difference of the technical phrafes in an indictment, fhall put a man into the peril of that *judicial difcretion*, which may fine him FORTY THOUSAND POUNDS, whether he has it or not, and commit him until it be paid? that is, in other words, WHICH MAY IMPRISON HIM FOR LIFE.

Since Mr. Hampden's trial, and foon after the Revolution, viz. in the 7th of Wm. 3. an act was paffed " for regulating trials in cafes of treafon,
" and mifprifion of treafon," wherein it was enacted, that every perfon

M

Mr. *Law*. I want to have the fact found—I pray it with the joint advice of some of the most learned persons in the profession, I mean Mr. Serjeant Hill THE ATTORNEY AND SOLICITOR GENERAL †.

Mr *Erskine*. Whatever opinion I may entertain upon the argument Mr. Law has offered to your Lordship, I will not controvert it here; but I shall insist on the twelve honourable gentlemen in that box, telling the people of England, whether aye or no, my clients ought to be convicted, after the testimony I am in the course of giving.

Mr. *Law*. I am equally before those gentlemen and the people of England, for the protection of the people of England; if you rise in this tone I can speak as loudly and as emphatically—I will prosecute these men with all the liberality of a gentleman, there

---

accused and indicted for high treason, or misprision of treason, should have a true copy of the whole indictment delivered to him five days at the least before his trial; and that no person should be indicted, tried, or attainted of high treason, or misprision of treason, but by and upon the oaths and testimony of two lawful witnesses, either both of them to the same overt act, or one of them to one, and the other of them to another overt act of the *same treason*. And that every person, who should be so accused, indicted, and tried, should have a copy of the panel of the jurors returned to try him, delivered to him two days at the least before his trial, and that no evidence should be admitted or given of any overt act, not *expressly* laid in the indictment. And by an act passed in the 7th of Anne, " for " improving the union of the two kingdoms," it was further enacted, that every person indicted for high treason, or misprision of treason, should have a list of the witnesses to be produced on the trial for proving the said indictment, and also a list of the jury, with the names, professions, and places of abode of the witnesses and jurors, together with a copy of the indictment; and that the same should be delivered to the party indicted, ten days before the trial, in the presence of two or more credible witnesses.

But these statutes are no longer a protection for the subject, if he may be proceeded against for a *conspiracy*, which is only another name for the same accusation, while it removes and destroys these salutary provisions and safeguards of the people.

It was unnecessary for Mr. Walker and the other defendants, indeed it would not have become them, to avoid the verdict of a jury, by resorting to any legal objections; yet if the doctrine laid down in the case of Hampden, be *at this day* law, how many innocent men, under a *state prosecution*, without any previous knowledge of the jurymen and their political partialities, may upon the PERJURY *of a single witness, be thus sent to prison for the rest of their days?* and where are the benefits of the acts of William and Anne, if they are to be evaded, under a precedent established before those acts were passed, in the most infamous times, and by the most iniquitous of judges?

† It seems not a little extraordinary that *the* ATTORNEY GENERAL *for the County Palatine of Lancaster* should pray *to let the fact be found,* upon a special verdict—that is, in other words, *to let Dunn's evidence be admitted as true,* though even *in this stage of the trial,* it had been *positively disproved* by so many respectable witnesses, and Dunn was (while in court) committed by the Judge for PERJURY. The defendants would by this means, have subjected themselves to be punished, as if they had been *actually guilty* of the crime they were accused of, although they were *perfectly innocent of every part of the charge,* and were in consequence HONOURABLY ACQUITTED.

is nothing has betrayed improper paffion on my part, but no tone or manner fhall put me down

Mr. *Erſkine*. I am not accufing Mr. Law of any impropriety or illiberality of conduct at all; I have faid nothing to that effect; for the only time in which I have named his name, or hinted at it, I have fpoken of him with refpect; nothing can be interpreted to the contrary: but a man, if he is not made of ftone, muft have fome feelings in a cafe of this fort. In whatever way your Lordfhip may rule this point, I fhall be fatisfied; I might have afked your Lordfhip's opinion early, but the fame reafon that induced your Lordfhip fo liberally and gracioufly not to communicate your own opinion, governed me.

Mr. Juftice *Heath*. You wifh it to go to the Jury.

Mr. *Erſkine*. Yes I moft certainly do.

Mr. *Walker*. I am before my country, and I will go to the Jury. In our fituation, even the delay of juftice, would be the height of injuftice.

Mr. *Law*. I cannot find it ftanding upon any authority, but a cafe in Dyer.

Mr. Juftice *Heath*. It has been always held that the mifdemeanor is merged in the felony.

Mr. *Erſkine*. When Mr. Law has heard the evidence out, for we have by no means done, if he fhould then think it becomes the Crown to go on, he will do fo, and then let the point of law be referved in any way moft agreeable to your Lordfhip; *but I will have the fact before the Jury*.

Mr. *Law*. If it ends in your clients' exculpation, I fhall be as happy as you; *but I fhall fee that it does fo*.

Mr. *William Seddon* (fworn).

Examined by Mr. *Erſkine*.

Q. Have you ever feen this man, Dunn, who has been examined to-day?

A. I have.

Q. How did it happen that you faw him?

A. Mr. Walker, Mr. Richard Walker, Mr. Duckworth, Mr. Jackfon, and myfelf, were upon bufinefs at my houfe, on Tuefday the 18th of December laft: I was particularly bufy in my office preparing for the affizes, but I was defired to come out upon a matter of moment. When I came into the houfe, I was told by Mr. Walker ———

Q. Did Thomas Dunn come?

A. No, not to my houfe; I went down to Mr. Richard Walker's with Mr. Duckworth; I ftayed there fome time: when I came there, I underftood Dunn was in the parlour with Mr. Walker, Mr. Richard Walker, Mr. Jones, and Mr. Ridgway, junior.

Mr. *Law*. What is the paper you are referring to?

A. Notes I took down at the time. Mr. Duckworth, Mr. Jones the attorney, and Mr. Ridgway the attorney, were with me at

Mr. Richard Walker's; but Mr. Ridgway and Mr. Jones were not present at any part of the conversation I am speaking to.

Mr. *Erskine*. Subsequent to this time, did Thomas Dunn, the man who has been examined to-day, come into the house?

A. He came the second time about eleven o'clock, Mr. Walker Mr. Duckworth, Mr. Richard Walker, and myself, were present—he knocked at the door, and came into the room; he first wanted to speak to Mr. Walker *alone*, or to Mr. Richard Walker: on being desired to speak, he repeatedly objected, and declared he would say nothing before so many witnesses; Mr. Walker told him he must speak before them, or not at all—he then desired Mr. Walker to sit along side of him, and he would esteem it an honour, and tell him every thing. Mr. Walker refused. Dunn then stood up, and desired Mr. Walker to give him his hand—I am just now informed that I said this happened on the 18th of December; if I did, I made a mistake, it was on the 18th of last month.

Q. Did you take these notes at the time?

A. I took down the latter part of the conversation, which I have not yet come to, from Dunn's own lips, I made a minute of this immediately after he was gone.

Mr. *Erskine*. Then I conceive, I am allowed to desire the witness to look at that paper to refresh his memory.

Mr. *Law*. How soon afterwards did you put it down?

A. This part *(the witness holding a paper in one hand)* the moment he was gone; the other *(shewing another paper)* I took from his own lips. Dunn stood up, and desired Mr. Walker to give him his hand, and he should esteem it a greater honour than if George the third did. This Mr. Walker again refused, and told him he had sworn falsely against him; Dunn acknowledged he had, and that he had not had a quiet night for thirteen weeks. He then rose from his chair, and threw himself upon his knees, and seized both Mr. Walker's hands, and exclaimed with a great deal of emotion, " I have done you injustice, and I beg your pardon," he then cried excessively, and addressing himself to the defendant Mr. Walker, said " My heart is almost broken, I am unhappy; I " have certainly done you wrong;" he then went down upon his knees to Mr. Walker again. Mr. Richard Walker then put this question to him, *Who instigated you?* Dunn replied, " *I am afraid* " *to tell that*, I have not slept a contented night these thirteen " weeks together, on your brother's account. Do not you know " I wished him well? I have lodged an indictment against him, " but it is a damn'd eternal falsehood." At this stage of the business he again cried very much, threw himself down upon a table, and was in an apparent agony for about ten minutes. When he recovered he seemed very composed and sedate, much more so than he was before. As soon as he lifted his head from the table, (after he had done crying) Mr. Thomas Walker asked him if he did not feel easier? to which he made no particular answer, but said, " The charge was taken down wrong at Manchester." Mr. Richard Walker then put this question to him, " How could you, " when you say you wished my brother so well, *be prevailed upon* " to accuse him so wrongfully?" to which Dunn answered, " that's " a very cross question." The same question was put again by

Mr. Richard Walker, to which Dunn said, "I want Mr. Walker to forgive me, and I will do him justice hereafter. I wish you would get a constable to take me up, and let *me* be tried." Mr. Walker then said, "you admit you have done me an injury?" to which Dunn replied, "yes, I have, every person knows it, except Yorke. What I swore in my first examination, and at Lancaster, were very different, not at all alike. I was called before the Grand Jury three times; I will never go to Lancaster at the assizes, and let Griffith and the rest of them do as they please, and be damned." Mr. Richard Walker repeated this question to him, "*Who instigated you to do wrong?*" Dunn said, "I won't answer such questions." I then asked him what day he had charged the offence as committed? His answer to me was, "between the 28th and the 30th of January 1793." Dunn then, of his own accord, speaking to Mr. Walker, said, "What shall I say to you, I have done you an injury, and I am sorry, what can I say more." I then said to him, "who set you on?" Dunn answered, "I know I behaved ill, I WAS BRIBED TO IT, THAT IS PLUMP; but I won't tell who did it, that shall for ever rest in my own breast." After the above conversation was ended, which I took down verbatim, in question and answer, Dunn left the room.

Thomas Dunn called up again.

Mr. Justice *Heath*. Well Dunn, have you heard this evidence; did that pass, or any part of it?

Dunn. No, nothing at all—yes, something of it passed.

Mr. Justice *Heath*. How much of it passed?

A. I went there *when I was intoxicated, the same as I am now.*

Mr. *Law*. Have you been out of the court?

A. Yes, I have.

Mr. Justice *Heath*. How long have you been intoxicated?

A. Not very long; I have my recollection about me, though it may seem to the court that I may be ill, or may not.

Mr. Justice *Heath*. Were you intoxicated when you gave your evidence just now?

A. I was not.

Mr. Justice *Heath*. You have been intoxicated since then?

A. Yes.

Mr. *Law*. How much of that conversation is true? there is some part you say is true?

A. I was at Mr. Walker's house about a fortnight hence; I went into Mr. Walker; I was brought in by a constable of Manchester, and upon that I met Mr. Richard Walker, brother to Mr. Thomas Walker.

Q. What is the constable's name?

A. One Twifs. Mr. Richard Walker asked me, Dunn, don't you recollect that you have done an injury to my brother? or to that purpofe; well, fays I, upon the firft examination I lodged the firft indictment againft him.

Mr. Juftice Heath. Has any body been with you, while you were out?

A. No.

Mr. Erfkine. I fhould be glad to trace where he has been—I don't believe he has been out of court.

Mr. Juftice Heath. Where have you been?

A. I have been down the town.

Mr. Serjeant Cockell. He was told to ftay in court.

Mr. Juftice Heath. Where did you dine?

A. Below the change; I don't know the houfe.

Mr. Juftice Heath. Is it a houfe you frequented before?

A. Yes.

Mr. Erfkine. Who dined with you?

A. The man's name is Fofter.

Q. Any body elfe?

A. Yes, Mr. Sidebottom.

Q. Who elfe?

A. Nobody.

Q. Who are Sidebottom and Fofter *?

Mr. Law. You fay Mr. Seddon and Mr. Duckworth were by at Seddon's houfe?

A. No, he was at Mr. Walker's; all that paffed, was this; he brought me, this Twifs, he intended to take me in, and to bribe me over; he gave me fome money upon it, on Mr. Walker's account, drunk or fober I will fpeak the truth.

Mr. Juftice Heath. I don't know how we can examine a man that is drunk.

Mr. Law. What was you to do for that money?

A. To go out of the way, and not appear here at thefe affizes.

Q. Did you beg Mr. Walker to fit along fide of you, and fay you would efteem it as great an honour as if George the third did?

A. I never faid, that upon my oath.

Mr. Juftice Heath. How can you Mr. Law examine him, after he has told you he is intoxicated? He has made himfelf fo exceedingly drunk, it is impoffible to examine him.

Mr. Erfkine. He denied pofitively he had ever been at Mr. Walker's, or was ever lured by any body to make a confeffion.

Mr. Law. Did you ever confefs that the charge you made againft Mr. Walker, was unfounded and falfe?

A. Never.

Mr. Erfkine. Then what this gentleman has faid, is falfe, is it?

A. I do not know, when was that?

Mr. Seddon. On the 18th of March.

Mr. Law. Did Twifs bring you there upon that occafion?

Dunn. Yes.

---

* *Fofter and Sidebottom were in the lift of witneffes for the Crown, delivered in Court at the commencement of the trial, by the attornies for the profecution.*

Q. Is he in any employ for Mr. Walker?
Dunn. He was employed five months upon this bufinefs.
Mr. *Erfkine.* Hear this read over, and ftand up, and remember you are in the prefence of God.

(Mr. William Seddon read his notes again.)

Mr. *Erfkine.* Is that true?
A. No, *I never entered into any part of the houfe, only the door, and which was juft opened for me.*
Mr. *Erfkine.* Mr. Seddon is fwearing falfely, is he?
A. I cannot tell what he may do; he is fwearing falfe, if he fwears that.
Mr. *Erfkine.* Did you go down on your knees, and cry for ten minutes?
A. You may as well tell me that I am a woman.
Q. Did you do that?
A. No, all he afked me, all I told him was this—Did not you lodge an information, fo and fo, and fome particular words; you were drunk; I faid, I will correct it next morning, *that is all that ever happened.*
Q. You never faid, you had wronged Mr. Walker, and went down upon your knees?
A. I never did.

Mr. *Duckworth* (called again.)

Crofs-examined by Mr. *Law.*

Q. Was you prefent, when this man, Dunn, anfwered the queftions put to him, in the manner Mr. Seddon has fworn juft now?
A. I was.
Q. To the beft of your memory and recollection, is the account that Mr. Seddon has given of it, the truth?
A. I looked it over, and it agreed with Mr. Walker's, Mr. Richard Walker's, and my recollection.

Mr. *Duckworth.*

Re-examined by Mr. *Erfkine.*

Q. I afk you—(though the attorney for Mr. Walker, you are a Chriftian, I truft)—I afk you in the prefence of God Almighty, is it true or falfe?
A. It is true.

Mr. *Duckworth*.

Cross-examined by Mr. *Law*.

Q. How came you all there, and how came Twiss to bring this man?

A. Mr. Thomas Walker and I had gone up to Mr. Seddon's. Mr. Jackson I think was there when I went in. Mr. Seddon was in his office. When we had been there a few minutes, Mr. Richard Walker came in, and said a message had been set to his house, that Dunn wanted to go to Barlow, to see his brother Mr. Walker: we agreed that Mr. Jones and Mr. Ridgway Junior, who had nothing to do with the prosecution, should be requested to be present to hear what passed. Mr. Seddon and I followed after.

Q. Do you think it professionally proper, when you knew that an indictment was found upon the testimony of this witness, and that he was to be the witness to sustain it at the next assizes, for you two, the attornies for the defendant, to have him alone with you, without any person on his behalf, and to examine him in this manner?

A. We thought it fitter that he should say what he chose to say, in the presence of some other person, than Mr. Seddon and myself; and, therefore, we desired Mr. Jones and Mr. Ridgway, two gentlemen of unimpeachable character, to be present. I did believe Dunn had perjured himself, from the knowledge I had of the cause; therefore, I thought it right, that what he chose to say, as a confession of his guilt, should be heard. When Mr. Jones, and Mr. Ridgway, had heard what he had to say, and had been gone from Mr. Richard Walker's about half an hour, there was a knock at the door, Dunn came in again alone, then Mr. Seddon and I, *from necessity*, and *not from choice*, went into the room.

Q. Had Mr. Jones and Mr. Ridgway taken his examination?

A. They had about half an hour before this time.

Mr. *Erskine*. Did you send for this man?

A. No.

Q. Did you employ any body to bring him to you?

A. No.

Q. But when a man had sworn falsely against Mr. Walker, you thought it right to hear his confession of his guilt?

A. I did—I thought he had perjured himself.

Q. Dunn says, that Twiss does work for Mr. Walker?

A. I never heard that he did.

Mr. *Walker*. Dunn said, Twiss was employed by me in this business.

Mr. *Law*. A man who is your fustian-cutter, is employed by you.

John Spink (sworn.)

Examined by Mr. Serjeant *Cockell*.

Q. Have you any acquaintance with Mr. Thomas Walker?
A. I have none at all.
Q. He is a gentleman who is a perfect stranger to you.
A. Yes, I only know him by sight.
Q. Have you any acquaintance or connection with him?
A. None at all.
Q. Do you know a man of the name of John Twiss?
A. Yes.
Q. I understand he and you are neighbours?
A. We are.
Q. Did you happen on the 18th of March 1794, to go to Twiss's?
A. I did.
Q. Was that matter of accident?
A. It was an accident.
Q. Who did you find at the house of Twiss?
A. I found Thomas Dunn.
Q. That man behind you?
A. Yes.
Q. Be so good as to relate what passed at that time.
A. Dunn said, he was sorry that he had injured Mr. Walker's character in the manner he had done; that he had never seen any thing that was bad by him. He asked me to go to Barlow-Hall with him that night, to see Mr. Walker.
Q. Did that request come from him to you?
A. It did; I told him I would not go with him at that time of night, but if he chose, I would go with him the next day; he said, no, he would see Mr. Walker before he slept, I said, he had better send to see whether Mr. Walker was in town, or not, to save him the labour of going. Esther Ottey went to see whether Mr. Walker was at home; she went to Mr. Thomas Walker's house in town, the servant told her he was in town, but he was gone out to tea and supper; when she came back, Dunn desired Esther Ottey and me to go to Mr. Richard Walker's; and see if he was at home.

Q. Did you, or did Twiss at this time, force the conversation, or was it entirely from himself?
A. He said it voluntarily of himself.
Q. Did you draw him on by any thing?
A. Not at all.——
Mr. *Erskine*. Speak up.
One of the *Jury.* It does not signify, we have been satisfied a long while.
A. I went out with Esther Ottey, to Mr. Richard Walker's; he said, if Thomas Dunn wanted to see him, he might come up in the course of half an hour, and he would let his brother know. I

suppose he did let him know. Esther Ottey went up to see if he was come in half an hour. He was not at home, she waited a little time,—then we took Dunn there, John Twiss and me, and left him at Mr. Richard Walker's door.

Q. Was he carried in custody at all?
A. No, he desired us to go with him.
Q. And you went and left him at Mr. Richard Walker's?
A. Yes.
Q. What time in the evening was this?
A. About nine o'clock, as near as I can guess; it might be half an hour before, or half an hour after.
Q. Did you observe, during the conversation you have been relating, whether Dunn appeared to be cool or was agitated?
A. He seemed very much to want to go.
Q. Did he appear to be much moved?
A. He seemed to be very much affected for doing what he had done—he seemed to relent.
Q. Was you in company, or did you see Dunn upon the 28th of March?
A. No, I saw him on the 20th.
Q. At what time of day?
A. About five o'clock.
Q. What passed then?
A. He was in at John Twiss's again, Twiss sent for me in, Dunn said he had seen Mr. Kinnaston, and he had challenged him with being acquainted with John Twiss, which he said he denied.
Q. Did you see whether he had cried; or observe any thing of that sort?
A. Yes, I saw tears in his eyes several times.

John Spink.

Cross-examined by Mr. *Wood*.

Q. You don't know how long he had been at Twiss's when you found him there on the 18th of March?
A. No.
Q. Nor how much liquor he had drunk?
A. No, I do not.
Q. Do you know whether he had drank any?
A. He had had a little, but he was quite sensible; he knew what he was saying and doing.
Q. Just as much as he knows now?
A. He was not half so much in liquor then as he is now.
Q. How came Twiss to have him in his care?
A. I suppose Dunn came to seek Twiss.
Q. What connection has Twiss with Mr. Walker?
A. I do not know that he has any.
Q. Is not he a workman of Mr. Walker?

A. I dare say he is.
Q. How long had he been after this man to get hold of him?
A. I cannot tell any thing about it.
Q. When you saw him again, he was with Mr. Walker's clerk?
A. On the 19th Dunn said Kinnalton had challenged him with being with Mr. Walker's clerk.
Q. Was he with Mr. Walker's clerk then?
A. He was; but I was not there till late in the evening.
Q. Was he drunk then?
A. No, as sober as I am now.
Q. Was it late?
A. It was about nine o'clock.
Q. He did not appear to have drank any thing?
A. He might have had some drink, but he was perfectly sober.

John Twiss (sworn.)

Examined by Mr. *Chambre.*

Q. You live at Manchester, don't you?
A. Yes.
Q. Are you one of the special constables of Manchester?
A. Yes.
Q. There have been several appointed within the town, two hundred, or thereabouts, I believe?
A. I do not know just the number.
Q. Do you know Dunn the witness, that has been examined?
A. I know this man Thomas Dunn.
Q. Were you with him on the 18th of March?
A. I was.
Q. How happened you to come together on that day?
A. Thomas Dunn called at my house; I was lying on the bed; I was sick; he came, and said he had a shilling to spend.
Q. You did not take him into custody?
A. No.
Q. It is not usual, is it, for people to come to a special constable for the purpose of being taken into custody?
A. I went along with him to Welch's; he began reflecting upon his bad conduct—that he had used Mr. Walker very ill.
Q. Did he begin of his own accord?
A. Yes, he did; he repeatedly said, he had used Mr. Walker very ill, that he was sorry for it, and would ask Mr. Walker's pardon. I said, if thou hast used him ill, thou hadst better ask his pardon in the public news-paper.
Q. Did he express any desire to see Mr. Walker?
A. Yes, he did, and he would see him, and he wanted me to go to Barlow-Hall with him, and he would pay my expences.
Q. How far is Barlow-Hall from Manchester?

A. I do not know—I was never there.—I said it was rather too late, if he would content himself, I would go with him in the morning.

Q. Was Spink with you at that time?

A. Spink was in my house, we came from Welch's; Spink came into my house, he desired Spink likewise to go along with him.

Q. Did you ever give him any money, or make him any promises, to induce him to say any thing upon the subject?

A. Never a farthing in my days but otherwise—I told him I would not, I never gave him a halfpenny in my life; I lent him thirteen shillings at different times—part of the money before I knew any thing about Mr. Walker's affair, that was on the 20th of October last, on a Sunday night; I lent it to him and Sidebottom, and they went and spent it; it was of a Sunday night.

Q. After that time, did you ever lend him any thing?

A. I lent him nine shillings since.

Q. When was the last time you lent him any money?

A. The last time was the 21st of March.

Q. How long before the 18th of March, had you lent him money?

A. I had never lent him a halfpenny, but four shillings.

Q. Had you lent him any thing between the 20th of October, and the 18th of March?

A. Not a halfpenny, nor never promised him any thing.

Q. You did not go with him to Barlow that night?

A. No—Dunn proposed to Esther Ottey, to go and see if Mr. Walker was at home—I was not taking every notice in the world. I think she said, I saw Mr. Walker in the town to-day, had not somebody better go and see if he is in Manchester? he desired her to go, she went, when she came back the information to the best of my knowledge was, she said Mr. Walker is gone out to supper, and it will be late before he returns. Upon this Dunn was determined he would see him he said before he slept; he sent her a second time, to go to Mr. Richard Walker, and John Spink and she went to the best of my knowledge; they returned back, and told him Mr. Richard Walker was at home, and Spink and me might bring him up; we went and brought him up, and left him at the door.

Q. Was all this done entirely upon his own solicitation, and at his own request?

A. Upon my oath it was at his own request, not one word of interrogation.

Q. Had you ever any sort of conversation with Mr. Thomas Walker?

A. I never spoke to Mr. Thomas Walker since he was born, but at one time; there was a fire at a new building at the bottom of Bridge-street; I did not see a constable, or any one assisting but myself; the gentlemen were beating up for the marine corps; Mr. Thomas Walker and Mr. Richard Walker came up, and a brutish kind of a man knock'd another man down in the sludge. Mr. Thomas Walker said to me, "do you know that man?" "I do not, "sir." That is every word I ever changed with Mr. Thomas Walker in my life.

Mr. *Erskine (to Dunn).* What do you say to this now?
Thomas Dunn. I say it is false, every word of it.

John Twiss.

Cross-examined by Mr. *Topping.*

Q. You are, I believe, a fustian-cutter of Mr. Walker?
A. By business, I am.
Q. How long have you worked for Mr. Walker?
A. I worked for Mr. Walker—that is, I work for Esther Ottey, and she has had work from that house for about six years.
Q. You was saying something about the ninth of January?
A. I have not told you aught about it yet.
Q. Was you with Dunn upon the ninth of January?
A. I was.
Q. Where?
A. At the White Bear, opposite the Infirmary; from thence we took a walk to Pendleton Pole.
Q. You was with him upon the ninth of January?
A. Yes, and the eighth likewise.
Q. Had you been drinking with him at both these public houses?
A. On the eighth I drank share of a pint of porter, and left him.
Q. How came you to be seeking his company, upon the eighth and ninth?
A. He fell into my company on the eighth; I had been at Liverpool, and delivered a message from Luke Foster, and that was the reason I saw him.
Q. Upon the 20th of October, or thereabouts, you had lent this man some money?
A. Four shillings.
Q. Had you any manner of knowledge of Dunn?
A. Seeing him last assizes here.
Q. And yet, upon the 20th of October, you lent him money?
A. Yes, I did; I have lent many a four shillings to different people.
Q. Having no knowledge of him, but what you had at the last assizes here, you lent him four shillings upon the 20th of October?
A. Peter Sidebottom was in company with me.
Q. You say you was at Liverpool; did not Dunn go from Manchester to Liverpool with you?
A. Not with me.
Q. You went after him?
A. No.
Q. Will you swear you never went to Liverpool after Dunn?
A. At what time?
Q. Will you swear you never went to Liverpool after Dunn?

A. I have been there after him, within thefe eight days—*with a fubpœna in my pocket to fubpœna him.*
Q. You was with him drinking upon the eighth and ninth of January?
A. Yes.
Q. Upon the 18th of March you was again with him at Welch's?
A. Yes; I told you he called upon me, and I went off the bed with him.
Q. Who was in company with you at Welch's?
A. John Spink, and me, and one James Stott.
Q. When you was with Dunn at this public houfe, do you remember Mr. Walker's clerk, Mofes Eadon, coming?
A. I do, but not upon the 18th.
Q. Was that upon the 19th?
A. Yes.
Q. And the 20th too, I believe you were drinking together?
A. I never faw him before the clofe of the evening of the 20th when he came to our houfe.
Q. Was Mofes Eadon, Mr. Walker's clerk, with you upon the 18th, or not till the 19th?
A. Upon the 19th.
Q. Upon Eadon's coming in, did not Eadon go into another room, and did not you tip Dunn upon the fhoulder, and defire he would go with you into another room?
A. I did.
Q. How much liquor had you together at this public houfe upon the 19th?
A. At this time we had had very little?
Q. How much money was fpent, before you parted?
A. I cannot poffibly tell.
Q. Don't you know, that fourteen or fifteen fhillings was fpent by Mr. Walker's clerk, at this meeting upon the 19th?
A. Mr. Walker's clerk never paid a penny to my knowlegde—I paid moft of it.
Q. You treated Dunn, did you?
A. I paid the fhot, and treated him.
Q. How much did you pay?
A. I cannot tell to a fhilling or two.
Q. Was it twenty fhillings?
A. No.
Q. Was it fifteen fhillings?
A. I cannot fay.
Q. Was it above half a guinea?
A. It was.
Q. Was it not fifteen fhillings?
A. It might be for what I know, I cannot tell.
Q. Did not you tell Dunn, you wifhed he would get out of the way, till the affizes were over?
A. Never, no fuch matter.
Q. You fwear, that at no time you ever told Dunn, you wifhed he would get out of the way, till the affizes were over?
A. Never in my days—I wifhed otherwife.

Q. Do you mean to swear upon your oath, that you did not advise him to remain at Preston?

A. I did not; he said, he would go to Preston, for he said he would not be subpœna'd by any party; of all things, I said, you will stand forth at the trial; he said, I will, but I will not be subpœna'd by any party.

Q. Upon the 19th of March he told you he would not be subpœna'd by any body?

A. That was on the 20th, and he said the same on the 21st in the morning.

Q. When did you lend him this other money?

A. I lent him one part on Wednesday night, somewhere about the 19th, and he had the remaining part some on Thursday, and the remaining part on the Friday morning.

Q. How much has he had in the whole from you?

A. Thirteen shillings, from the first to the last.

Q. And all this, after this meeting at Weleh's the Hare and Hounds?

A. No, he had only nine shillings then.

Q. Have you never received from any person whatever, either the money that you spent at the Hare and Hounds, or the money you lent Dunn?

A. I have not upon my oath.

Q. Nor no promise?

A. Nor no promise of any thing. Dunn promised he would pay me my money back again.

Q. You never had, from any other person living, a promise of re-payment of the money lent?

A. No, never.

Q. Have you never received any money back that you spent?

A. No, never, from man, woman, nor child.

Q. Mr. *Erskine (to Mr. Duckworth).* When you heard that it was reported, that this Dunn had run away, and was not coming to the assize, did you take any step in consequence?

A. I had heard he was gone to Preston, and would stay there till the assizes. We were much afraid he would run off. I went to Preston to desire Mr. Cross, the *prothonotary*, would devise some means of keeping him in his custody by a bailiff, or in some other manner. Mr. Cross would not do that, but advised me to subpœna Dunn; we sued out a subpœna, and endeavoured to serve him with it. Mr. Twiss was sent to Liverpool, to endeavour to subpœna him there. He could not be found. It had been reported that we had bribed Dunn to keep out of the way.

Mr. Justice *Heath*. I cannot think there is much in the thirteen shillings, *for if Dunn was so corrupt that thirteen shillings would influence his testimony, his credit is not worth much.*

Mr. *Thomas Jones* (sworn).

Examined by Mr. *Lloyd.*

Q. Was you at Mr. Walker's on the 18th of March?
A. I was.
Q. Was Dunn, the man who stands behind you, there?
A. Yes, he was, he came soon after I got there.
Q. Did you hear him say, he had sworn true or false, against Mr. Walker? what did he say about Mr. Walker?
A. When he first came into the room, he seemed as if he was rather intoxicated. I thought he reeled across, from the door towards the window; he sat himself down, and in a little time a question was proposed, I think by myself; Whether he had not something to say to Mr. Walker? he said he had wronged Mr. Walker. I asked him in what manner he had wronged Mr. Walker? *he said he had accused him falsely.* Immediately as he said that, *he fell down upon his knees, and begged his pardon.* Mr. Walker desired him to get up. Several other questions were put to him, in what manner he had falsely sworn against Mr. Walker, he did not give any answer to them.
Q. Was he brought into the room by force, or did he appear of his own free will?
A. I understood he came of his own free will; he knocked at the door, and was introduced into the room; *he said,* HE HAD BEEN BRIBED TO DO WHAT HE HAD DONE.
Q. Did he seem affected—was he in tears?
A. He seemed very much agitated when he entered the room. I asked Dunn, *who had bribed him,* he would not give me an answer to that question.

Mr. *Jones.*

Cross-examined by Mr. *Law.*

Q. Was Mr. Twiss, the constable there?
A. He was not there. The persons present in the room, when I was there, were Mr. Walker, Mr. Richard Walker, Mr. Ridgway the attorney, myself, and Dunn.
Q. I only wanted to know whether Twiss was there; you need not mention who were there, for the purpose of confirming what you say. Did he seem to you, so far recollected at the time he talked with you, as to be aware of the import of what he was saying?
A. Yes, I thought he was, perfectly?

Q. Did he specify any particulars, in which he had accused Mr. Walker falsely?

A. He did not; I asked him that question; he did not give an answer to it; he seemed very desirous of communicating what he had to say to Mr. Walker *alone;* he seemed very loth to say any thing to any questions put to him, while Mr. Ridgway and I were there; he frequently desired that Mr. Walker and he might confer together; Mr. Walker did not choose to trust himself with him alone.

Q. You have no sort of doubt in your recollection, that Dunn used those words that he had accused Mr. Walker falsely?

A. He did.

Q. Was there any conversation, respecting the indictment that was depending at Lancaster at that time?

A. I did not hear any thing said about an indictment. There was a question put to Dunn, either by Mr. Walker or Mr. Ridgway, I believe, by Mr. Ridgway, whether he had ever heard Mr. Walker damn the King? *he said, he never had,* he had heard him speak disrespectfully of him. I asked him in what manner he had spoken disrespectfully of him? but to that question he gave no answer.

Q. Was there any mention made at that time, of any assemblies held at the house of Mr. Walker, for the purpose of exercising with arms?

A. Not a syllable?

Q. Was any thing said of Mr. Yorke being at Mr. Walker's? be so good as tell me all that passed at that meeting?

A. There was a question asked about Mr. Yorke; it was asked by Dunn himself—instead of directly answering Mr. Walker's questions, he seemed to evade them by putting the question whether Mr. Yorke had been in town or no? or whether he had seen him within a few days? Mr. Walker did not give him any answer to that question.

Q. Nothing was said then about Yorke's having been at the meeting at Mr. Walker's house?

A. No.

Q. How long might Dunn be with you in the whole?

A. I fancy he was about twenty minutes, or half an hour in the room—the questions I have mentioned, were frequently put to him.

Q. Did you take any thing down in writing of what passed?

A. I did that night when I got home.

Q. Have you a minute of it?

A. I have.

Q. Be so good as to let me look at that minute; it is not from any doubt of your giving me the best of your recollection, I wish to see it for another purpose.

(*Mr. Jones gave Mr. Law his minutes.*)

You mention here, I see, that you went with Mr. Richard Walker, Dunn was soon introduced—by whom was he introduced?

A. I think Mr. Richard Walker shewed him into the room, if I recollect right; somebody knocked at the door very soon after we got there; I understood it was Dunn; he came immediately into the room.

Q. Who introduced him?

A. I think Mr. Richard Walker opened the door when Dunn came into the room. I was doubtful towards the end of the business, whether he was drunk, *or only feigned to be so;* for towards the latter end of it he appeared more steady, and seemed *perfectly collected* in every thing he said; he was particularly urgent with Mr. Walker to be *alone* with him. Finding that could not be obtained, he wished to be with the two Walkers; that was refused; then he desired he might be with Mr. Richard Walker *alone*, which was also refused, and Mr. Walker peremptorily told him he would not suffer himself to be in his company *alone*. The man seemed very much vexed at it and he came out with a threat upon the occasion; he said Mr. Walker would repent of it, *for it would be a damn'd deal worse for him, let him bring as many witnesses as he would.*

Mr. *Erskine.* Mr. Thomas Dunn, is this true or false?

A. *False.*

Q. This gentleman is perjured then—it is all false?

A. *Yes.*

Mr. *Law.* I know the character of several of the gentlemen who have been examined, particularly Mr. Jones; I cannot expect one witness alone, unconfirmed, to stand against the testimony of these witnesses; I ought not to expect it.

Mr. Justice *Heath.* You act very properly, Mr. Law.

The Jury immediately gave their verdict NOT GUILTY.

Mr. *Vaughan.* I pray that Dunn may be committed.

Mr. *Erskine.* We will undertake to prosecute him for PERJURY.

Mr. Justice *Heath.* Let him be committed; and I hope, Mr. Walker, that this will be an admonition to you, to keep better company in future.

Mr. *Walker.* I have been in no bad company, my Lord, except in that of the wretch who stands behind me; nor is there a word or an action of my life, in which the public are at all interested, that I wish unsaid, or undone, or that under similar circumstances I would not repeat.

Mr. Justice *Heath.* You have been HONOURABLY ACQUITTED, Sir, and the witness against you is committed for PERJURY.

Immediately after the above verdict was given, the same jury was again impannelled, and sworn to try Mr. WALKER upon the *separate* indictment, charging him with *damning the King, and saying, he would as soon take his head off, as tear a bit of paper.*

Thomas Dunn, the only evidence for the CROWN on this indictment, having been committed for PERJURY, the Jury instantly returned their verdict, NOT GUILTY.

Mr. Walker had the most incontrovertible evidence to prove, *he was in London at the time Dunn swore that the words laid in this indictment, were spoken by Mr. Walker in Manchester.*

The jury were again impannelled and sworn to try JAMES CHEETHAM, upon the *separate* indictment against him, for *damning the King, and wishing he was guillotined*; but the witness for the CROWN, Mr. Dunn, having been committed for perjury, the jury IMMEDIATELY found the defendant NOT GUILTY.

Upon Saturday, the 5th of April 1794, a Bill of Indictment was preferred againſt THOMAS DUNN, for PERJURY; and found by the Grand Jury, of which the following is a Liſt.

Thomas Butterworth Bayley, Eſq. of *Hope*, Foreman.
Nicholas Aſhton, Eſq. of *Woolton*.
William Aſheton, Eſq. of *Cuerdale-Lodge*.
Edward Buckley, Eſq. of *Lancaſter*.
Daniel Bayley, Eſq. of *Hope*.
Joſeph Brookes, Eſq. of *Everton*.
Charles Gibſon, Eſq. of *Lancaſter*.
Geoffry Hornby, Sen. Eſq. of *Preſton*.
John Fowden Hindle, Eſq. of *Blackburn*.
Henry Hulton, Eſq. of *Preſton*.
Robert Heſketh, Eſq. of *Lancaſter*.
John Machell, Eſq. of *Pennybridge*.
Thomas John Parke, Eſq. of *Highfield*.
Edmund Rigby, Eſq. of *Grange*.
Abraham Rawlinſon, Eſq. of *Ellel-Hall*.
William Rawlinſon, Eſq. of *Ancoats*.
Nicholas Starkie, Eſq. of *Frenchwood*.
Robinſon Shuttleworth, Eſq. of *Preſton*.
Henry Sudell, Eſq. of *Blackburn*.
John Walmeſley, Eſq. of *Preſton*.
James Whalley, Eſq. of *Clark-Hill*.
Joſeph James Vernon, Eſq. of *Preſton*.

APPENDIX.

No. I.

Copy of Mr. Walker's first Letter to Mr. Secretary Dundas.

Bate's Hotel, 17 June, 1793.

SIR,

I HAVE been for some time absent from home, on account of business which has required my presence in London. I find by my letters of last Saturday, (the contents of which are still more strongly confirmed by those of to-day) that a report has been *industriously circulated* in Manchester of a charge of HIGH TREASON, made against me, before the magistrates of that town.

I am extremely sorry to occupy your time with the frivolous rumours that idle and ignorant, or bigotted and malevolent people may amuse themselves with propagating at the expence of my character. But the report above-mentioned is in itself so serious, and has been the topic of so much conversation at Manchester, that I think it right, in justice to myself, and to obviate *any false construction* which my enemies may put upon my absence from home, to inform you, Sir, that my residence is as above-mentioned, and that I shall be not merely *ready and willing*, but *desirous* to meet any charge that may be made against me from whatever quarter it may proceed. I shall be upon change at the usual time almost every day this week, and I shall be this evening in the lobby of the House of Common, or in the gallery there.

I have the honour to be,
Sir,
Your most obedient servant,

(Signed) THOMAS WALKER.

The Right Honourable Henry Dundas,
Principal Secretary of State for
the Home Department, &c. &c.

No. II.

Copy of Mr. Walker's second Letter to Mr. Secretary Dundas.

Bate's Hotel, 22d June, 1793.

SIR,

IN consequence of *repeated* advice from Manchester of warrants *for* HIGH TREASON having been issued against me, I thought it right to inform you by letter on Monday last, that I resided during my stay in town, at *Bate's Hotel*, and that I should be at the House of Commons on that evening, and on change at the usual hours almost every day of the week. I have kept my promise.

I confess I am somewhat surprized, under all the circumstances of my situation, that I have not been favoured with an answer to that letter, but had the business rested there, I should probably have troubled you no further.

By a letter, however, from my attorney in Manchester, sent yesterday under cover to a friend of mine, I learn officially that a warrant upon a charge of HIGH TREASON has certainly been issued against me at Manchester, and I have every reason to suppose (if my information be true) that the *intent* of the charge in the first instance, and the subsequent delay in proceeding upon it, is not to punish me for a political offence, of which I know I am not guilty, *but to injure my general character and reputation;* indirectly indeed, but irrevocably.

The character and credit of a commercial man, Sir, is too delicate to be trifled with. Hitherto mine has been unsullied; and I trust it will remain so by any conduct of my own. But the principle of harrassing a British merchant *by vague reports, industriously circulated, of crimes he has never committed; by charges unfounded, and threats unexecuted,* is so base, so detestably malignant, that I hope, for the honour of the national character, it is confined to my enemies at Manchester.

It is highly improbable that any charge of so criminal a nature, can have been made against me, without its being known to the office of his Majesty's secretary of state. I do, therefore, earnestly entreat, that I may be kept no longer in suspense; that I may be treated forthwith according to law, if there be any legal accusation against me, or if there be none, that I may be informed of it without delay. I think I have a right, after what has passed, to require as an act of common justice, that my mind may be set at ease, and that I may be enabled to attend to my commercial concerns, without the perpetual anxiety attendant upon reports and suspicions most injurious and unfounded.

Mr. Wharton will do me the favour to deliver this, and wait for an answer*.

In the mean time I am,
Sir,
Your obedient servant,

(Signed)   THOMAS WALKER.

The Right Honourable Henry Dundas,
his Majesty's Principal Secretary
of State for the Home Department,
&c. &c.

---

* While Mr. Wharton went in to Mr. Dundas, Mr. Walker, and Mr. Cooper as his friend, waited near the door of the Board of Controul, till Mr. Wharton came out.

APPENDIX.

No. III.

Copy of a Letter from Mr. Walker to Mr. Wharton.

Bate's Hotel, London, 15th July, 1793.

DEAR SIR,

 I HAVE no doubt you will be much surprized, when I inform you, that I am still without any answer to the letter you did me the honour to take to Mr. Dundas (as secretary of state for the home department) upon the 22d ult. and several of my friends, being not less surprized than myself at the silence of Mr. Dundas, are anxious to know what passed between you and him upon the delivery of my letter. I shall, therefore, consider myself particularly obliged, if you will favour me, as nearly as you can recollect, with the substance of the conversation which took place on that occasion.

With much respect and esteem believe me,
 Dear Sir,
 Very sincerely your's,

   (Signed)   THOMAS WALKER.

John Wharton, Esq; M. P. Skelton
Castle, near Guisborough, Yorkshire.

No. IV.

Copy of Mr. Wharton's Answer to Mr. Walker.

DEAR SIR,

 I AM much surprized to find that you have not yet heard from the secretary of state's office in reply to the letter I delivered from you to Mr. Dundas, on the 22d ult. The conversation that passed between us on that occasion, you desire that I should repeat to you; it is impossible for me to undertake to do it verbatim; but the substance was, that I presented the letter at your request, in consequence of your not having received any reply to one of a similar purport, that you had written to him on the preceding Monday; and that being kept in a state of suspense on a subject of so serious a nature, was highly injurious to you as an Englishman and a merchant.—Mr. Dundas read the letter, and said that it was impossible for him to make any other reply to it than this, that he received serious and criminal charges against you; that he had consequently taken such steps as his official duty required, to have those charges investigated, and that I might assure you, that no official delay should arise, and that when any determination was taken respecting them, you should be apprized of it. I said you wished for nothing more than a speedy determination on the steps to be taken, and that you did not wish to escape the justice of your country, if you had offended it; and I added, that you had accompanied me to his office, and that I was ready to deliver up the culprit, if he considered you as such, immediately;

APPENDIX

but I apprehended that upon a full inveftigation of the charges againſt you, it would appear that perfonal enmity to you, and jealoufy of your commercial connections, had inftigated perfons who had failed in their attempts to injure you commercially, to make this attempt to take away your life; Mr. Dundas faid it was poffible that there might be low and perfonal motives for the profecution, and that he (from every thing he had heretofore heard or known of you) had too good an opinion of your underftanding, to fuppofe you would fubject yourfelf to the penalties of high treafon. I then thanked him for his candour and politenefs, and took my leave.

I fhall be very happy to hear from you, if any thing further is done in this bufinefs, and remain,

      Dear Sir,
    With great regard, your's, very fincerely,
      (Signed)   JOHN WHARTON.

Skelton Caftle, July 21, 1793.

Thomas Walker, Efq; Bate's Hotel,
 Adelphi, London.

No. V.

Copy of a third Letter from Mr. Walker, to Mr. Secretary Dundas.

            Bate's Hotel, 29th July, 1793.

SIR,

 FROM Mr. Wharton's account of the converfation that paffed between you and him, on his delivering to you my letter of the 22d ult. I was induced to expect an early intimation of the intended proceedings againft me, or of their having been relinquifhed, I fhould be much furprized that no decifion had yet taken place on this bufinefs, if I were not confcious that the more ftrictly the accufations were inveftigated, the more futile they would appear.

 My bufinefs in London will occupy me till Sunday next, when I fhall fet out for Lancafhire, unlefs fome notice from the office of his Majefty's fecretaries of ftate fhould detain me longer in town.

      I have the honour to be,
        Sir,
       Your moft obedient fervant,

       (Signed)   THOMAS WALKER.

The Right Honourable Henry Dundas,
 his Majefty's Principal Secretary
 of State for the Home Department,
 &c. &c.

APPENDIX.

Mr. Walker not having received an answer from Mr. Dundas to any of his three letters, and judging that Mr. Dundas's testimony might be essential, directed him to be subpœnaed to appear as a witness on his trial at Lancaster. The following are copies of two subpœnas with which Mr. Dundas was served, together with the copies of two letters, the one from Messrs. Ward, Dennetts and Greaves, agents to Messrs. Duckworth and Dennett, and the other from Mr. White, solicitor to the treasury, to Messrs. Ward, Dennetts and Greaves, upon this subject.

No. VI.

Copy of the first Subpoena with which Mr. Dundas was served.

GEORGE the third, by the grace of God, of Great-Britain, France, and Ireland, King, Defender of the Faith, &c. To the Right Honourable Henry Dundas, our Principal Secretary of State for the Home Department, greeting, we command you, that laying aside all other business, excuses, and delays whatsoever, you be and personally appear before our justices at Lancaster, the first day of the next general session of assizes of oyer and terminer, and general gaol delivery there to be holden, to testify and speak the truth between us and Thomas Walker, George M'Cullum, John Smith, William Paul, Samuel Jackson, James Cheetham, Oliver Pearson, Benjamin Booth, Henry Yorke, and Joseph Collier, on the part and behalf of the said Thomas, George, John, William, Samuel, James, Oliver, Benjamin, Henry, and Joseph, upon all such matters and things whereupon you shall be examined; and that you bring with you and produce upon the said trial, three several letters, purporting to be written by the said Thomas Walker to you, one of which is dated in the words and figures following, "Bate's Hotel, 17th June, 1793," and is signed and subscribed with the name "Thomas Walker," and is directed to you by the description of the Right Honble. Henry Dundas, Principal Secretary of State for the Home Department, &c. another of which said letters is dated in the words and figures following, "Bate's Hotel, 22d June, 1793," and is signed and subscribed with the name "Thomas Walker," and is directed to you by the description of "The Right Honble. Henry "Dundas, his Majesty's Principal Secretary of State for the Home Department, &c. "&c." and the other of which said letters is dated in the words and figures following. "Bate's Hotel, 29 July, 1793," and is signed and subscribed with the name of "Thomas Walker," and is directed to you by the description of "The Right Honble. "Henry Dundas, his Majesty's Principal Secretary of State for the Home Department, "&c. &c." And this you are not to omit, under the penalty of one hundred pounds. Witness, Sir Archibald Macdonald, Knight, at Lancaster, the 15th day of August, in the thirty-third year of our reign.

BATT.

(Endorsed)

March 24th, 1794. Served this subpœna on Mr. Dundas, at his house at Wimbledon, and at the same time offered him thirty guineas, which he refused.

(Signed) J. DENNETT.

No. VII.

Copy of the second Subpoena with which Mr. Dundas was served.

GEORGE the third, by the grace of God, of Great-Britain, France, and Ireland, King, Defender of the Faith, &c. To the Right Honble. Henry Dundas, our Principal Secretary of State for the Home Department, greeting, we command you, that laying aside all other business, excuses, and delays whatsoever, you be and personally appear before our Justices at Lancaster, the first day of the next general session of assizes of oyer and terminer, and general gaol delivery there to be holden, to testify and speak the truth between us and Thomas Walker, George M'Cullum, John Smith, William Paul, Samuel Jackson, James Cheetham, Oliver Pearson, Benjamin Booth, Henry Yorke, and Joseph Collier, on the part and behalf of the said Thomas, George, John, William, Samuel, James, Oliver, Benjamin, Henry, and Joseph, upon all such matters and things whereupon you shall be examined; and also that you bring with you and produce upon the trial of this traverse, all informations and examinations, taken on oath or otherwise, of Thomas Dunn, or any other person or persons against the said defendants, or any of them, either for high treason, conspiracy, or any other crime or misdemeanor, transmitted and delivered to you, either as the Secretary of State, or otherwise, and all warrants, or copies of warrants issued thereon."—And this you are not to omit under the penalty of one hundred pounds. Witness, Sir Archibald Macdonald, Knight, at Lancaster, the fifteenth day of August, in the thirty-third year of our reign.

BATT.

(Endorsed)

Served this subpœna, by delivering a copy to Mr. Nepean, who undertook to accept it as if served on Mr. Dundas.

(Signed) J. DENNETT.

No. VIII.

Copy of Messrs. Ward, Dennett and Greaves's Letter to Messrs. Duckworth and Dennett.

The King against Walker and others.

GENTLEMEN,

WE could not get to see Mr. Dundas to serve the last subpœna upon him, but Mr. Nepean received it, and he undertook to accept it as good service,

vice, since which we have received the inclosed letter from the Solicitor to the Treasury, which admits the service of both subpœnas.

We are,
Dear Sirs,
Your's, sincerely,
(Signed) WARD, DENNETTS & GREAVES.
Covent-Garden, March 27, 1794.

We return you the subpœna.

Messrs. Duckworth and Dennett,
Manchester.

No. IX.

Copy of Mr. White's Letter to Messrs. Ward, Dennett and Greaves.

The King against Paul and others.

SIRS,

THE subpœna which you served on Mr. Dundas, requiring him to produce three letters, sent by Mr. Walker, one of the defendants, to Mr. Dundas, as Secretary of State, hath been sent to me, together with Mr. Walker's letters.

I beg leave to acquaint you, that these letters shall be produced on the Trial, if called for, and I will instruct his Majesty's Counsel to admit that they were received by Mr. Dundas, in his capacity of Secretary of State, and that both subpœnas have been served.

I am,
Sirs,
Your most humble servant,

(Signed) JOSEPH WHITE,

No. 6, Lincoln's Inn,
27 March, 1794.

Messrs. Ward, Dennetts and Greaves,
Soliciters, Covent Garden.

No. X.

Particulars of several Applications made by Mr. Richard Walker, respecting his Brother, Mr. Thomas Walker, to the Rev. John Griffith, one of his Majesty's Justices of the Peace.

ON Thursday July 18th 1793, I went to the Rev. John Griffith's house a little before ten in the morning, accompanied by Mr. William Seddon, but finding Mr. Griffith was gone to church, we waited in the church-yard till he came out, when Mr. Seddon told him we wanted to speak to him, on which Mr. Griffith took us into a public house in the church-yard, where Mr. Seddon informed him that as we understood he had granted a warrant against Mr. Walker, we came to let him know that Mr. Walker was in London, and where he was to be met with; that he (Mr. Griffith) might get the same served upon him there. Mr. Griffith replied, *that there certainly was a warrant signed by him against Mr. Thomas Walker, for* HIGH TREASON, and when he came home, it would be put in force; that there had been a person *waiting in the* MARKET-PLACE* *to apprehend him*, at a time when it was reported he was returned home, that Unite, a deputy constable, had either been at Barlow or in the neighbourhood, as it was said Mr. Walker had been there, and that he had also been seen in Manchester. I told him it was perfectly untrue; that my brother had never been out of London or the neighbourhood, since he first went up; Mr. Griffith said " I do not hesitate to declare *that as the matter now stands we cannot convict either Mr.* Paul *or any other person of high treason* as we have only one witness at present." I then read him the annexed paper, and gave him my brother's address on a card, in my brother's own hand-writing. Mr. Griffith said, he did not see why he should act out of his own district, and that I had better give the card to Unite, who had the warrant, and might do as he pleased; I replied, I should have nothing to do with Unite, or any such people, that he (Mr. Griffith) had declared he had granted a warrant for my brother's apprehension, and therefore I left the card with him. He persisted in saying, he saw no reason for his acting; Mr. Seddon replied, he thought *if Mr. Walker had been really guilty of* HIGH TREASON, *he ought to have been taken up, or to be so immediately, wherever he was*, and prosecuted at the expence of the public. Mr. Griffith said, he did not see that: *he had sent copies of the informations to government, and could not tell why they did not act*, and why they seemed to wish, *to throw the business on a country justice*. Mr. Seddon declared he thought it very strange, and a most malevolent piece of business throughout, and observed, that had a warrant been issued against any person on a charge of bastardy, he (Mr. Griffith) would have taken care to have it backed, and the person apprehended at the charge of the parish. Mr. Griffith replied, *" that would be for the security of the parish."* Mr. Seddon said, " true, and this being on a charge of high treason, is for the security of " the kingdom, and ought to be at the expence of the public." Mr. Griffith still said, they had only one witness; on which I remarked, that with all the pains which it was reported he, the Rev. Mr. Griffith, had taken, it was surprizing he could not get another witness *as good as the one they had*, but that I thought no candid or dispassionate person was at a loss to what motive to attribute the present proceedings. I also mentioned my brother's having given notice to Mr. Dundas, of his having been in London.

The Rev. Mr. Griffith said, " that so far from his acting in London, was he there, " and had a sufficient acquaintance with Mr. Thomas Walker, he should not think it
unjustifiable

---

* *The Market-place in Manchester is considered as the Exchange, where the merchants and manufacturers meet to transact their business.*

APPENDIX.

"unjuſtifiable or improper to call on him at his own hotel, and dine with him." On which Mr. Seddon ſaid, *What!* DINE WITH A TRAITOR! and I added, *and one againſt whom you yourſelf have iſſued a warrant for his apprehenſion!* he replied, "I mean as a private gentleman;" we both repeated, *would you dine with a* TRAITOR?"

Mr. Griffith then ſaid, it was not incumbent on him to take any ſteps to apprehend Mr. Thomas Walker out of his own neighbourhood, on which Mr. Seddon obſerved, that the warrant being for conſpiring or compaſſing the death of the King, *as he (Mr. Griffith) had acknowledged*, and Mr. Thomas Walker being in London ſo near the King's perſon, he might more eaſily have an opportunity of putting his wicked intentions into execution, but that a traitor ought to be taken into cuſtody wherever he was as ſoon as poſſible; and I ſaid, *it ſhewed little regard for the ſafety of the King's perſon, to ſuffer thoſe who were accuſed of conſpiring againſt his life, to be at large ſo near him without interruption.*

The Rev. Mr. Griffith alſo declared, that Unite had *followed Mrs. Jackſon's Funeral to have apprehended Mr. Jackſon, had he followed her to the grave;* that he wiſhed Unite not to interrupt the ceremony, as he thought it would be *rather indelicate,* but to follow Mr. Jackſon, and take him up *as he returned home,* or at his own houſe. Mr. Griffith alſo ſaid, he was perſuaded that treaſon had been actually committed at Mr. Walker's houſe, but that *Mr. Walker was not preſent at the time.* I replied that was not the fact, for neither my brother, nor I, had any connection with people guilty of treaſon. Mr. Griffith ſaid, it had been reported he had an indemnity from government for what he had done, but that was not the caſe.

Mr. Seddon mentioned Mr. Paul's treatment, and Mr. Griffith's having refuſed a copy of the information, and the reports which had been ſo ſhamefully ſpread, reſpecting different people being apprehended here for high treaſon, and that the matter ought certainly to be brought to a concluſion. After repeating the general purport of the paper alluded to, and Mr. Griffith again declaring that he ſhould give the card to Unite, who might act as he thought proper, we left him.

I again went on the 31ſt of July, with Mr. Birch and Mr. Sanderſon, to Mr. Griffith, and gave him notice in their preſence that my brother would be at Lancaſter at the enſuing aſſizes.

On the 5th of Auguſt I again informed Mr. Griffith, that my brother would be in Mancheſter on the Thurſday, or Friday following; Mr. Griffith aſked where he would be, to which I replied, that I could not tell preciſely where he would be, but that he would be in Mancheſter; Mr. Griffith ſaid, "WILL HE BE UPON CHANGE?" I ſaid, "*Why ſhould he be upon change?*" he will be in Mancheſter." Mr. Griffith further aſked, " Will your brother pledge himſelf to take his trial *for* " *ſedition* at the enſuing aſſizes? for *I have two* charges againſt him for HIGH TREA-" SON, and another for *ſedition.*" I replied, "he will be in Mancheſter at the time " I mention, on Thurſday or Friday next."

On Thurſday my brother returned from London to Barlow, and on Friday morning he came to Mancheſter, of which I gave Mr. Griffith immediate notice.

RICHARD WALKER.

No. XI.

Copy of the Paper read by Mr. Richard Walker, to the Rev. Mr. John Griffith, upon the 18th of July, 1793, in the Preſence of Mr. William Seddon.

I UNDERSTAND from the information of ſeveral reſpectable perſons, that there is a warrant out againſt my brother Mr. Thomas Walker, ſigned by you, on a criminal charge of ſome kind or other; my brother has received the ſame information: as this report is now generally current in Mancheſter, I think it right to acquaint you, that my brother Mr. Thomas Walker, refides at prefent at Bate's Hotel, in the Adelphi, London; that his bufinefs will detain him in London fome time; that he wifhes himfelf, and! with on his account, that no uncertainty refpecting the place of his abode, m. y delay the courfe of juftice; and therefore if there be any warrant againft him, you may have the opportunity of getting it properly backed, and ferved upon him without delay, as he will certainly remain in London a fufficient length of time to enable this to be done. He is generally upon the Royal Exchange every day at the ufual hours.

If there be no charge againft my brother, I think I have a right to call upon you to fay fo, as my commercial reputation is involved, as well as his, in the prefent reports againft him. That you may not pofsibly make any miftake, I give you this card, with his addrefs in his own hand-writing.

(Copy of the Card.)

Mr. Walker,
of Manchefter,
Bate's Hotel,
Adelphi,
London.

18 July, 1793,
about 11 o'clock,
A. M.

No. XII.

Copy of the Paper referred to in the Evidence of George Clark.

To the Reforming Societies in Sheffield, and other perfons who concur with them in fentiment.

ALLOW a fincere well-wifher to the liberties of mankind, and particularly to the happinefs and freedom of this country, moft earneftly to exhort you, his fellow-townfmen to continue to teftify, by the whole of your behaviour, that "the true fpirit of liberty is a fpirit of order," as your Society for Conftitutional Information has well expreffed it. Be this your invariable method of refuting and defeating the numerous calumnies of thofe who, from miftaking your views, or other motives, mifreprefent your real defigns. You may be affured that nothing will chagrin fuch as are your enemies, fo much as to find that you keep fteadily, on all occafions, to a ftrict obfervance of the laws, and a peaceable conduct; nor would any thing gratify them more, or be fo effentially injurious to the caufe of that Reform which you wifh to obtain, than for you to be fo far milled as to commit any act of riot or tumult.

Promote with firmnefs, by all juft, legal and peaceable means, a Reform in the Reprefentation of the People, maintain the freedom of the Prefs—that indifpenfable fafeguard to your Liberties—and affent, in the like calm and peaceable way, your right to free difcuffion on political fubjects. But at the fame time do all th's with propriety and difcretion. Do nothing which can be conceived by others *except from wilful perverfion*, to be inimical to that Conftitution, one branch of which you profefs it to be your defign to reftore to its due purity by conftitutional renovation.——Where events happen favourable, as you think, to juft and univerfal liberty, avoid public rejoicings and proceffions, becaufe they may prove offenfive inftead of conciliating to thofe of your fellow-citizens who do not view fuch occurrences in the fame light that you do; becaufe they may affoard your opponents, and thofe who wifh you ill, an opportunity to excite confufion and diforder; whereby the perfons or property of your neighbours might be injured, which would be laid to your charge, though you might be quite clear of any intentional harm, and becaufe they may, from examining caufes attending fuch proceffions and rejoicings, be conftrued into an infult on the Government of your own country, notwithftanding you may mean nothing of the kind.

APPENDIX.   xi

Leave all tumult and disturbance, all injury to those who differ from you either in Politics or Religion, to men of a very different description from yourselves—to men who level the property and endanger the persons of innocent and meritorious citizens, for exercising the right of private judgment, to those who oppose all Reform, to those who are zealous for acknowledged abuses. To such men as these let it be left to prove themselves the only *levellers* to be found in this country.——How contrasted is the spirit of such men, to that liberal one of moderation and social intercourse, which happily prevails among persons of all opinions in this town and neighbourhood!

As no instance of outrage and violence can be justly alledged against the friends of Reform during the late and still existing alarms, do you carefully support that honorable and peaceable character. Manifest to all that you do not entertain the levelling principles you are charged with, by a constant regard to the safety of the persons and property of all around you.—Protect, but do not destroy. Bear reproach with manly firmness, but do no injury yourselves. Convince by peaceable behaviour, by obedience to legal authority, and by that dignity of conduct which is becoming those who are influenced by the principles of genuine Liberty.

Your townsmen and neighbours, at their meeting this day, have done nothing unfriendly to Liberty or Reform, but have expressed a confidence in the peaceable disposition of the inhabitants of the town. It is your part to continue to shew that you are worthy of that confidence. They have declared their firm attachment to the Government and Constitution of their country, one grand principle of which is to amend what may be amiss, from the lapse of time or other circumstances; and their abhorrence of all riot and tumult, with a resolution to assist the civil magistrate in quelling every thing of that nature. These declarations are agreeable to the sentiments contained in some of the publications of your Society for Constitutional Information. In confirmation of which, one of the members of that Society gave his approbation to the proceedings of the meeting in a manner highly to his credit; and the general concurrence as well as the handsome behaviour of the others who attended, ought not to pass unnoticed.

Permit me to add a few words more.—What is the object of Political Reform, but by suitable regulations to guard more effectually against oppression, to produce more general comfort and happiness, to prevent future unnecessary burdens on the subject, and gradually, as well as rationally, and with due respect to safety as well as justice, to diminish those which already exist. To the industrious, economical, regular and orderly mechanic, such a reform would become an essential benefit as he could then by moderate but constant labour, enjoy more comfort, maintain his family better, and be able to provide a sufficiency for sickness and old age; but to the idly disposed, the profligate and drunken workman, on the supposition of his continuing to be so, it could be of no advantage.

May I then further urge upon you the necessity of letting personal amendment go hand in hand with Political Reform and Information. When you examine the errors of Government, do not forget to cast an eye upon your own failings. These you may correct by sincere efforts, for this is within your own power. Your endeavours to reform the other, though also laudable, may not be certain of success. However you will be much more likely to succeed in public reformation, when you have abandoned whatever is degrading to your own characters. From your general behaviour, let no one be able to point out a Reformer, or a member of one of your Societies, without at the same time he should point to an industrious, regular man, of sober manners, and an orderly, peaceable disposition. By being meritorious servants, good masters, kind husbands, and provident fathers, you will acquire a respectability which will conquer the prejudices of those who now traduce your intentions. These are means by which you may indeed put yourselves on an *equality* with men in higher stations, and but too frequently become their superiors, in real worth and usefulness, in actual comfort and enjoyment, and by the possession of true independence. This should be your ambition, and in this may you succeed, both in self-reformation, and, united with your fellow-citizens, in that of the representation of the People, to the extent that will most conduce to individual, as well as to public happiness and prosperity, is the cordial wish of

          (Signed) A REFORMER.

December 31, 1792.

The sentiments contained in the above paper, were so much approved by the Manchester Constitutional, Reformation, and Patriotic Societies, that they unanimously directed two thousand copies to be printed and distributed.

No. XIII.

WILLIAM PAUL

IS a paper-ftainer in Manchester. On the 14th of June, 1793, he was torn from his wife and family, in confequence of a warrant figned by the Rev. John Griffith, charging him with HIGH TREASON, " by compaffing the death of his prefent Majefty," on the fole cath of Thomas Dunn; Mr. Paul was that day and night confined, in an apartment belonging to the New Baily Prifon; the next morning he was committed to that prifon, and orders were given to treat him as a common felon.—— Upon the 17th of the fame month, a commitment was made out for him to the Caftle at Lancafter; but fome days being allowed him to fettle his books, &c. he was not fent there until the 23d, when he was taken out of his cell at one o'clock in the morning, without any previous notice.

Mr. Paul remained in the county gaol at Lancafter, till the enfuing affizes in Auguft, when no indictment for HIGH TREASON being preferred againft him, he was difcharged. Many of Mr. Paul's friends were ready to have given bail; but as in cafes of treafon, no bail can be taken, it is hardly neceffary to obferve, that by thefe means a man may be confined from the clofe of one affizes to the commencement of another, on an accufation of this crime; and although it requires two witneffes to convict a man, one only is fufficient to have him committed.

Mr. Paul being indicted at the Auguft affizes, for a confpiracy with Mr. Thomas Walker, and others, he was held to bail with the other defendants, and with them *honourably acquitted* in April laft.

During the time which Mr. Paul continued in the New Baily Prifon, neither his wife nor his children were permitted to fee him, without fome of the keepers being prefent; and he was forced to fleep in one of the cells of the felons, which having been frefh wafhed, there being no glafs in the windows, and the window fhutter much broken, gave Mr. Paul a cold, which afterwards terminated in a violent inflammation in his eyes, one of which he was in the greateft danger of lofing; he was confined to his bed for three weeks, and to his room for near three months.

This defendant has a wife and four children.

No. XIV.

Copy of the Warrant by which Mr. Paul was apprehended.

Lancashire, to wit. To the conftables of the townfhip of Manchefter, in the faid county, and to each and every of them.

YOU are hereby required, in his Majefty's name, to apprehend and bring before me John Griffith, clerk, one of his Majefty's juftices of the peace in and for the faid county, William Paul, of Manchefter, in the faid county, paper-ftainer, to anfwer to fuch matters as are and fhall be objected againft him, for having committed HIGH TREASON in the townfhip of Manchefter aforefaid, by compaffing the death of his prefent Majefty. And alfo for divers contempts againft our faid Lord the King. Given under my hand and feal; the 13th day of June, one thoufand feven hundred and ninety-three.

JOHN GRIFFITH, (L. S.)

No. XV.

Copy of Mr. Paul's Commitment to Lancaster.

Lancaster, to wit. To the constables of the township of Manchester, and also to the gaoler, or keeper of his Majesty's gaol the Castle of Lancaster, in the said county.

THESE are in his Majesty's name to require and command you the said constables, to convey the body of William Paul, of Manchester, in the said county, paper-stainer, to his Majesty's Gaol the Castle of Lancaster, and him there to deliver to the gaoler, or keeper thereof. He, the said William Paul, being charged before me on the oath of Thomas Dunn, with having committed HIGH TREASON, by compassing the death of the present king, at the township of Manchester aforesaid. And you the said gaoler, or keeper of the said gaol, are hereby required to receive into your custody in the said gaol, the said William Paul, and him there safely keep, until he shall be thence discharged by due course of law. Given under my hand and seal, at the township of Manchester aforesaid, the seventeenth day of June, one thousand seven hundred and ninety-three.

JOHN GRIFFITH, (L. S.)

No. XVI.

SAMUEL JACKSON.

THIS defendant being informed that a warrant for HIGH TREASON was issued against him, as well as against Mr. Walker and Mr. Paul, remained with his family who were in the country about five miles from Manchester, on account of the dangerous state of health of his wife, and whose death was greatly accelerated by her anxiety on this occasion. He, however, immediately, on receiving the information, desired his solicitors, Messrs. Duckworth and Dennett, to give notice to the Rev. John Griffith, the magistrate who was said to have issued the warrant, and to his clerk, and also to the agents to the solicitor for the prosecution, that if the warrant was for a bailable offence, he would instantly give bail, or if not, he would appear to meet the charge at the assizes; which notice was accordingly given; and his solicitors were informed that the charge was for HIGH TREASON.

After the death of Mrs. Jackson (in the beginning of July,) at whose funeral in Manchester, the deputy constable attended by order of the above magistrate, for the purpose of apprehending Mr. Jackson, he still remained in the country, though going about publicly, visited by his friends from Manchester, and the place of his residence known to Mr. Griffith.

On the 19th of July, his solicitors gave written notices to the Rev. John Griffith, and to his clerk, and also to the agents to the solicitor for the prosecution, that this defendant would attend at the following assizes, to meet any charge that might be brought against him; and on the 7th of August his brother gave another notice in writing to Mr. Griffith to inform him, that he (the defendant) would be in Manchester the next day, and the day following. On the 8th of August, Mr. Jackson came to Manchester, and the next day sent a message to the magistrate, to let him know where he was; but not being apprehended, he accompanied Mr. Walker to the assizes at Lancaster on the following day; when the charge of HIGH TREASON being abandoned, and a bill for a conspiracy found by the Grand-Jury, he gave bail with
the

the other defendants, to try the same at the following affizes, and was with them *honourably acquitted.*

To the affertion which the Attorney General for the county palatine of Lancaster was instructed to make in his opening on the trial, and which was afterwards attempted to be substantiated by Dunn, in his evidence, that the works of Paine, and many other works of a similar tendency, were read by this defendant to the societies; he has only to observe, that the whole is untrue.

No. XVII.

JAMES CHEETHAM

IS a hatter in Manchester. He was committed on the 23d day of July 1793, to the New Baily Prison, by the Rev. John Griffith, on the oath of Thomas Dunn, for speaking contemptuous words of his present majesty. He expected to be tried at the same time (viz. at the ensuing quarter sessions) with Benjamin Booth and Oliver Pearsall, both of whom were charged with expressions almost word for word the same, but instead of being brought to trial as he expected, for which he was fully prepared, and had incurred the necessary expences, he was, without having any previous notice, or being permitted to send to his wife or friends, removed at one o'clock in the morning of the 25th of July, to Lancaster Castle, where he continued till the assizes following, being imprisoned more than three weeks.

Although there was a vacant bed in the room where he lodged the night of his arrival at Lancaster, he was removed into another room the night after, where he was obliged either to sleep upon the floor, or in the same bed with the common hangman.

He was indicted at the assizes in August 1793, for *damning the King*, and also for the foregoing conspiracy, and was bailed on both charges. At the assizes in April last he was *honourably acquitted* of the latter indictment, with the other defendants. The former for which he had been committed, no evidence was brought in support of.

No. XVIII.

OLIVER PEARSALL

IS a native of Kidderminster, in Worcestershire, and by trade a weaver.— He came to Manchester in June 1792, for the purpose of working in the manufactures there. Upon the 31st of December 1792, he became a member of the Reformation Society, by which means Thomas Dunn came to know him. In March following he left Manchester, and returned to Kidderminster.

On the 29th of June 1793, the wife of Dunn, accompanied by one Parker, who Pearsall since learned was a constable, and Callaghan an Irishman, came to him at Kidderminster; Dunn's wife pretending it was necessary for him to give evidence at Manchester, on behalf of her husband, who she said was in the New Baily Prison upon *a false accusation,* and would rather see him (Pearsall) than receive five hundred pounds, as his evidence would clear him. This Pearsall declared himself ready to comply with, and went with them to a public house, where he was told, he should have all his expences paid, and should return back on the Wednesday following.——
Previous to setting off, Pearsall wanted to go home to get some cloaths, which Parker refused, and then said, he had some tackling (meaning handcuffs) in his pocket, which he would put on him if he was saucy; Parker never shewed any warrant, and repeatedly refused to take Pearsall before a magistrate, though several times asked to do so. On his arrival at Manchester, he was carried before the Rev. John Griffith, who
welcomed

APPENDIX. xv

welcomed him to Manchester, and asked him if he did not belong to the Reformation Society, to which he answered in the affirmative. Mr. Justice Griffith then questioned him if he had not seen *arms* in Mr. Walker's house, and if he had not *exercised men* there, to both which he answered in the negative. He was then carried to the New Baily Prison, where he was kept till the 5th of July, when he was committed, and remained there till the 9th of August.

While in this prison, Parker, Dunn, and Callaghan, had frequent interviews with him, the two latter instigating him to depose "to having seen arms, and to ha ing exercised men at Mr. Walker's." Callaghan in particular desired him to come forward in the cause, and confirm what Dunn had been putting to him, observing, if he did not, it would be the worse for him. The day after this, one of the deputy constables came to him, and asked him, whether he recollected what Dunn had said the night before? Pearsall replied, he recollected what Dunn had said very well, but that it was impossible for him to recollect things which had never happened. The constable then said, *that he had frequently seen the shining of firelocks in Mr. Walker's ware house, as he returned home late in the evening;* and further said, that a person was come from Yorkshire, and had sworn to the truth of what Dunn had said; that he was *paid twelve guineas* and had returned home with the money. Pearsall answered to this, "If he has sworn falsely, I cannot, for my soul is concerned."

In one of these conversations, Dunn said, Pearsall seemed uneasy at the interrogations; that they would leave him for the present, and begged him to consider of it. Pearsall said, he could not consider on a false subject, when Dunn replied, "we will drop the subject of exercising the men," and then began to talk about a letter from the Irish to the Scotch.

At other times, Callaghan and Dunn came to him, giving him the same advice; the former telling him, that if he did not confirm Dunn's testimony, Dunn was going to swear HIGH TREASON against him, which Dunn confirmed.

He was also informed that if he would join Dunn, *it would be as good as a pension to him as long as he lived.* At this conduct Pearsall grew angry, and desired them to leave the room; on which they said, *if he would not acknowledge these things, they wished he was at home again.*

On Thursday the 4th of July, Callaghan and Dunn came to him again, and brought pipes and tobacco, and a quantity of liquor. He was desired to drink, and smoke freely, to keep up his spirits, which he refused. One of them informed him, *that the Rev. Justice Griffith would come to the prison that night, and take his examination.* Accordingly about seven o clock the Rev. John Griffith came, with pen, ink, and paper. Mr. *Griffith shook hands very familiarly with Dunn, clapped him on the back, he was an honest fellow.* Mr. Griffith asked if their liquor was out, and seeing it was, he threw down a shilling, and ordered the turnkey to fetch some more, which was done; when it came, the Rev. Mr. *Griffith drank with them,* and afterwards asked Pearsall, whether he recollected *any thing relative to the questions Dunn had put to him;* to which Pea.fall said, *that he could not,* on which they all lent the room.

On Friday evening the Rev. Mr. Justice Griffith, came again to the prison, and examined Pearsall as before, who answered *that he knew nothing of the kind,* the Justice then told him, that Dunn had sworn *against him* (Pearsall) for having *damned the present King* in his (Dunn's) house; and therefore, that his commitment should be made out immediately, which was done accordingly.

Before Pearsall was committed by Mr. Griffith, he had of the best to eat and drink, but *afterwards* he had *only the jail allowance.*

At the ensuing quarter sessions in July 1793, Pearsall gave notice of his intention to take his trial on the indictment found against him, on the charge of having *damned the King.* The same day was fixed for the trial of him and Booth. The expences of the attorney and counsel were incurred, and every thing prepared for the trial, when the defendant was informed, *that by a process called a Certiorari, this indictment was removed from the sessions into the Court of King's Bench, but was given to understand that it was not intended to be proceeded on.*

The defendant, Pearsall, was notwithstanding this, detained in prison until Friday the 9th of August,¹ when Mr. Griffith wanted him to give bail for his appearance in the King's-Bench. This being refused by his solicitor as illegal, and an application being made by him to the clerk of the peace, for a copy of the magistrates' names attending the sessions, for the purpose of making an application to the Court of King's-Bench, to compel the magistrates to do their duty ;—the Rev. John Griffith sent to let Pearsall know that he might be liberated without bail, *upon his entering into*

into a recognizance to appear to the indictment in the King's-Bench. Pearfall entered into the *recognizance*, and was liberated. Purfuant to his recogizance, he appeared in the King's-Bench, and pleaded *Not Guilty*.———The iffue was made up, but although two affizes have fince elapfed, *the profecutors have not thought it expedient to try him upon this indictment*.

At the affizes in Auguft 1793, Pearfall went to Lancafter as a witnefs, *to prove the attempts which had been made to fuborn him to give falfe evidence againft Mr. Walker*.———Dunn s evidence being ftill unfupported, and likely to be deftroyed by this witnefs, the profecution againft Mr. Walker for HIGH TREASON was dropped;— and Pearfall was *prevented from giving evidence*, by being made a defendant in the indictment for a confpiracy. He was then bailed, and afterwards *honourably acquitted*.

No. XIX.

BENJAMIN BOOTH.

ON the fifth day of June 1793, this defendant was apprehended by virtue of a warrant iffued by the Rev. John Griffith, upon a charge of having diftributed a paper on the fubject of WAR, which paper *was alledged to be feditious*: for this charge he was bailed upon the 10th of that month, and about eleven o'clock on the very fame night, he was again taken from his wife and children, under *another warrant*, figned by the *fame reverend magiftrate*, and was the next day committed by him to the New Bailey Prifon, on the oath of Thomas Dunn, on a charge of having *damned the King*, and faying, *he would guillotine him if he could*.

At the door of Mr. Griffith's houfe, a perfon who had been prefent during Booth's examination, faid to the conftable who was taking him to prifon, " *Expofe him to the fury of the populace*." The conftable led him through the moft public ftreets in the town, and frequently addreffed himfelf to the mob, in very inflammatory language refpecting Booth.

The Rev. John Griffith refufed in the moft pofitive terms to admit this defendant to bail (which was offered), and he was confined in the New Bailey Prifon until the 19th of that month, when Mr. Griffith thought proper to receive bail*.

During the greater part of this interval Booth was kept in a feparate place, he was locked up two hours fooner, and let out of his cell two hours later than the reft of the prifoners. The threats and temptations held out to induce him to confirm Dunn's evidence, were various and frequent. He was told that others had done fo, and that he had but a few hours to determine whether he would or not, that otherwife he would moft certainly be hanged, and that it was the only way to fave his wife and children from ruin. Mr. Paul (then in confinement, fee the Appendix, No. xiii.) was fhewn to him at one of the windows in another part of the prifon. Booth was informed that Mr. Paul was committed for HIGH TREASON, that Mr. Walker, and others, had fled from the accufation; that in treafon there were no acceffories, all were principals; and that *if he would turn King's evidence* without delay, and join Dunn, Mr. Griffith would write for his *pardon*.

The Rev. Mr. Griffith told Booth, " *he wanted the great men, he wanted to pick " his birds*."

At length, by promifes and threats, by being told the parties accufed were either apprehended, or had fled from the charges againft them, and being frequently reminded of the helplefs fituation to which his wife and children would be expofed, a promife was wrung from him to join Dunn's evidence.

Upon Booth ftating his ignorance of what evidence Dunn had given, Dunn and he were put together, that Dunn might inform him; and orders were given that Booth fhould now be better treated, and have a moderate allowance of liquor, *but not fo as to make Dunn jealous*.

Booth

* The bail infifted upon and given, was Booth in 500l. and two fureties in 250l. each.

APPENDIX. xvii

Booth being afterwards bailed, an indictment was preferred against him at the enfuing quarter feffions, on the accufation of having *damned the King* &c. and immediately meeting the charge, *though he might have traverfed to the following feffions*, he was tried and found guilty on the *fore* teftimony of Dunn, although Dunn was flatly contradicted by Mary Booth, the defendant's fifter, who was prefent when the words were *faid to be fpoken*, and fwore pofitively they were made ufe of *by Dunn himfelf, and not by her brother*.

No indictment was preferred upon the firft accufation, of diftributing the paper, *pointing out the evils which were likely to refult from the war*.

It is remarkable, that Dunn accufed five or fix different people of ufing *precifely the fame expreffions* refpecting the King, at different times, and when not in company with each other.

The Chairman of the Manchefter quarter feffions in paffing fentence obferved, that Booth had been guilty *to the fatisfaction of the whole bench*, and the judgment of the court was twelve months imprifonment in Lancafter Caftle.

Benjamin Booth, thus imprifoned, was *again indicted* for the *confpiracy* with the other defendants, at the next affizes, and with them *acquitted* on the trial. At the period of his acquittal, *more than nine months* of his imprifonment had elapfed.

Benjamin Booth being thus indicted, both at Manchefter and at Lancafter, was effectually precluded from giving evidence of the practices made ufe of, *(whilft he was in prifon,)* to prevail upon him to give *falfe teftimony* againft fome of the other defendants.

It is perhaps not unworthy of remark, that *the Chairman of the Manchefter quarter feffions*, fhould afterwards be one of the grand jury who found the bills of indictment againft the defendants in this trial; he was likewife foreman of the Grand Jury who found the bill of indictment againft *Dunn for* PERJURY.

So well aware were the profecutors, of the mode in which Booth's declaration, in fupport of Dunn's evidence, *had been extorted from him*, (which he never reflects upon but with fhame and contrition, and which he acknowledges to be utterly falfe) that they did not produce it on this trial, nor did it prevent the Crown from granting Booth a pardon.

After Dunn (whofe conduct was reprobated by the whole court) was commited for perjury by the judge of affize, *the chairman of the Manchefter quarter feffions wrote* (it is faid) as well as the ATTORNEY GENERAL *for the county palatine of Lancafter*, to the Secretary of State, for Benjamin Booth's pardon.

On the 2d of May laft Booth was fet at liberty, in confequence of a pardon, of which the following is a copy,

No. XX.

(L. S.) GEORGE R.

Whereas Benjamin Booth was at a quarter feffion of the peace held at Manchefter, tried and convicted of fedition, and is now in Lancafter gaol under fentence of imprifonment for the fame; and whereas *fome favourable circumftances* have been humbly reprefented unto us in his behalf, inducing us to extend our grace and mercy unto him, and to grant him our free pardon for his faid crime. Our will and pleafure therefore is, that you caufe him the faid Benjamin Booth to be forthwith difcharged out of cuftody, and for fo doing this fhall be your warrant. Given at our court at James's, the twenty-fifth day of April 1794, in the thirty-fourth year reign.

To our trufty and well-beloved the
Chairman of the Quarter Seffions
of the Peace at Lancafter, the High
Sheriff of the faid county, and all
others whom it may concern.

By his Majefty's command,

(figned) HENRY DUNDAS.

Benjamin Booth has a wife and four fmall children.

On the 4th of October 1793, Benjamin Booth, while in Lancaster Castle, received a letter from Mr. Cartwright, of Shrewsbury, who is a surgeon and apothecary, and a Nonjuring Bishop, of which the following is a copy. The reader will make his own reflections upon its objects and principles.

No. XXI.

Copy of Mr. William Cartwright's Letter to Benjamin Booth, Dated Shrewsbury, 27 Sep. 1793.

When you wrote to me, soon after the death of Bishop Price, I little suspected that ever I should have seen your name in the public papers, on such an occasion as that which has rendered you so conspicuous; and reduced you to that situation, which your criminal conduct has so justly deserved.

I begin this adress to you in this manner, with no other design than to express my abhorrence and detestation of those principles which excited you to this conduct; for which the laws of your country are now punishing you; and which, without sincere repentance, leaves you obnoxious to the just judgment of the Almighty, whose holy laws you have so flagrantly violated, and thereby brought a scandal on that sound branch of the catholic church, of which you were a member.

You well know, or once did know, that unfeigned allegiance, in all civil matters, to your rightful and lawful Sovereign, is an essential doctrine and duty of christianity; and that all coercive resistance to him and his laws, *in all cases whatsoever,* and *under the most trying circumstances, is threatened with* DAMNATION.

I am quite at a loss to conceive on what ground you can possibly justify or excuse your late conduct. Sure I am that before you could adopt the maxims and principles of PAIN, and such men, you must either have made shipwreck of faith, and virtually renounced all reverence for the revealed will of God; or lulled your conscience into a very irreligious degree of torpor.

I thought I had sufficiently exposed the atheism of Pain's wicked book in that paper of mine signed "Phileleutherus Christianus," which was printed and dispersed in Manchester as a hand bill in May 1791.

I grant you there is much plausible reasoning in Pain's writings; many unfavoury truths, mixed with vile falsehoods, and gross misrepresentations: but his reasoning is entirely of that sort, with which the adversary of souls always endeavours to deceive the unwary. However, it is such as can have no influence, but upon those who have first withdrawn their minds from that dependance upon God, which is always our duty, and best security against the temptations of Satan, the allurements of the world, and the corrupt propensities of our fallen and depraved nature. The *unsavoury truths* disseminated in his writings are such as, more or less, exist in all governments in the world, and ever will, till there shall be an entire renovation of the fallen sons of Adam. The speculations of those who call themselves Philosophers, promise us mighty fine things indeed. But the world was not created by human wisdom, neither can it be reformed by such measures as those of Thomas Pain. *Reformation is a fine word; yea, and a good thing too, when properly set about:* but the experience of once should surely teach us the folly as well as wickedness of all popular attempts at it. Let every individual strive to reform himself, and leave the rest to God. While he is doing this, he is in the way of his duty: but whoever attempts to reform his superiors and the governing powers by the arm of flesh, will only fall from one wickedness to another, and will not come into the way of righteousness.

Possibly you may deceive yourself with a notion that you were doing right, in endeavouring to overturn the present established system of government, *because some of our religious predecessors attempted, in the years 1715 and 1745 to dethrone the then reigning family.* But give me leave to tell you that those attempts, whether *right or wrong,* whether justifiable or not, were undertaken on entire different and opposite principles, to those, on which you must have engaged with the new disturbers of the public

APPENDIX.

public peace. The former attempts were not undertaken to overturn or alter the conſtitution of the government of this country. No! It was a competition between a claimant to the throne, who was thought to have been unjuſtly and illegally diſpoſſeſſed of his right, and him who withheld that ſuppoſed right from him. That competition, you well know, is now at an end. The one family being as good as entirely extinct, and the other having been ſo long a time in uninterrupted poſſeſſion, *ſurely we need not now heſitate which of theſe God has choſen to reign over us.* He has declared "by me kings reign." And I believe there is not *now* one perſon of our communion who does not recognize King George as the only lawful King of Great Britain, &c.

In conſideration of this unqueſtionable truth, and of your late ſeditious and rebellious practices, it is my duty however painful, to tell you *that you lie under the cenſure of* THE GREATER EXCOMMUNICATION. The conſequences of ſuch a ſtate I need not explain to you, any further than to tell you that without an *examplary repentance there can be no pardon for you either in this world or* THAT WHICH IS TO COME. *By an examplary repentance,* I mean not only a ſincere contrition, ſuch as is deſcribed in the CXLth. leſſon, page 400, of our catechiſm, but alſo the moſt effectual reſtitution and ſatisfaction, which it may be in your power to make to that government which you have inſulted, and the laws which you have violated. And this can no other way be done, than *by diſcloſing to a proper magiſtrate, every thing which you know of ſeditious and rebellious plots; and endeavouring, not for the ſake of revenge or malice, but for the ſake of juſtice, and better ſecurity of the public peace, to bring all your aſſociates in iniquity, to ſuch puniſhment as the law preſcribes.*

Thus have I faithfully admoniſhed you, in love to your ſoul and body too, and delivered my own ſoul on this occaſion. I pray God to give you a right underſtanding in theſe, and all things concerning your eternal welfare, and am

   Your faithful but afflicted paſtor and friend,

     (ſigned) *WILLIAM CARTWRIGHT.*

I ſhall ſend this to you under the cover of a frank, directed to an old, ſenſible, and very worthy friend of mine; whom I have not ſeen for above twenty-three years laſt. His name is Langſhaw, now organiſt of Lancaſter. I ſhall requeſt him to give you the moſt efficacious advice he can; I am perſuaded it will be good and friendly; and I believe him to be as capable of convincing you of thoſe deluſive errors, into which you have fallen, as I am. If you have a due ſenſe of your crimes, it will give me ſome conſolation to receive a letter from you; otherwiſe not.

I believe it is not permitted to perſons in your ſituation to ſend or receive letters, without the inſpection of the governor, and I have no objection that he ſhould ſee this; I ſhall ſend it unſealed to Mr. Langſhaw.

To Mr. Benjamin Booth
 Lancaſter Caſtle.

THE END.

www.ingramcontent.com/pod-product-compliance
Lightning Source LLC
Chambersburg PA
CBHW020126170426
43199CB00009B/658